T(

I HE BASICS

The planning of urban and rural areas requires thinking about where people will live, work, play, study, shop and how they will get about the place, and to devise strategies for long time periods. *Town Planning: The Basics* provides a general introduction to the components of urban areas, including housing, transportation and infrastructure, and health and environment, showing how appropriate policies can be developed. Explaining planning activity at different scales of operation, this book distinguishes between the "big stuff", the grand strategy for providing homes, jobs and infrastructure; the "medium stuff", the design and location of development; and the "small stuff" affecting mainly small sites and individual households.

Planning as an activity is part of a complex web stretching way beyond the planning office, and this book provides an overview of the many components needed to create a successful town. It is invaluable to anyone with an interest in planning, from students learning about the subject for the first time to graduates thinking about embarking on a career in planning, to local councillors on planning committees and community boards.

Tony Hall is Emeritus Professor of Town Planning at Anglia Ruskin University, Chelmsford. Originally a transport planner, he later retrained in urban design focussing on design guidance. He served as a councillor for Chelmsford and led its planning policy for 7 years, culminating in the award of Beacon Status in 2003. He was with Griffith University, Brisbane, Australia, from 2004 to 2016. His 2010 book on the disappearance of Australian backyards won the 2012 PIA National Award.

THE BASICS

The Basics is a highly successful series of accessible guidebooks which provide an overview of the fundamental principles of a subject area in a jargon-free and undaunting format.

Intended for students approaching a subject for the first time, the books both introduce the essentials of a subject and provide an ideal springboard for further study. With over 50 titles spanning subjects from artificial intelligence (AI) to women's studies, *The Basics* are an ideal starting point for students seeking to understand a subject area.

Each text comes with recommendations for further study and gradually introduces the complexities and nuances within a subject.

THE QUR'AN (SECOND EDITION)
MASSIMO CAMPANINI

RESEARCH METHODS (SECOND EDITION)
NICHOLAS WALLIMAN

SEMIOTICS
DANIEL CHANDLER

SPECIAL EDUCATIONAL NEEDS AND DISABILITY (THIRD EDITION)
JANICE WEARMOUTH

SPORT MANAGEMENT
ROBERT WILSON AND MARK PIEKARZ

SPORTS COACHING
LAURA PURDY

TRANSLATION
JULIANE HOUSE

TOWN PLANNING
TONY HALL

For a full list of titles in this series, please visit www.routledge.com/The-Basics/book-series/B

TOWN PLANNING

THE BASICS

Tony Hall

Routledge
Taylor & Francis Group

NEW YORK AND LONDON

First published 2020
by Routledge
52 Vanderbilt Avenue, New York, NY 10017

and by Routledge
2 Park Square, Milton Park, Abingdon, Oxon, OX14 4RN

Routledge is an imprint of the Taylor & Francis Group, an informa business

Library of Congress Cataloging-in-Publication Data
Names: Hall, Tony, 1944 March 27- author.
Title: Town planning: the basics / Tony Hall.
Description: New York: Routledge, 2020.
Identifiers: LCCN 2019018936 (print) | LCCN 2019019176 (ebook) |
    ISBN 9780367257491 (e-book) | ISBN 9780367257477 (hardback) |
    ISBN 9780367257484 (pbk.)
Subjects: LCSH: City planning.
Classification: LCC HT166 (ebook) | LCC HT166 .H3542 2020 (print) |
DDC 307.1/216—dc23
LC record available at https://lccn.loc.gov/2019018936

ISBN: 978-0-367-25747-7 (hbk)
ISBN: 978-0-367-25748-4 (pbk)
ISBN: 978-0-367-25749-1 (ebk)

Typeset in Bembo
by codeMantra

CONTENTS

FIGURES

INTRODUCTION

WHAT IS THIS BOOK ALL ABOUT?

The purpose of this book is to try to explain to the general, non-professional, reader what the content of town and country planning really is. It is not a book about law and procedure. Although there is a real need for books that explain such matters, their shelf life is very short as, unfortunately, legislation changes all the time. What this book aims to do is give an idea of the kind of issues that planners have to grapple with and the basis on which they make their decisions. Hopefully, this will also give an insight into their day-to-day professional life and how their activities affect ordinary people. It is focused primarily on Britain but, by avoiding detailed legal matters, it may also be of use to those in other countries.

WHAT IS THE PROBLEM?

Why should town and country planning need explaining? There can often be a stark contrast between the importance of planning decisions in people's lives, as shown by their reaction to matters that affect them, and their lack of knowledge of the profession itself. They often have little appreciation of what is it and how is it organised.

Surely, some may say, a significant proportion of the population is affected by, and may get involved in, the local planning process. What can, indeed, be striking is the large attendances in the public gallery for planning committee meetings, compared to other local council committees, and the wide range of people who often attend. The fervour which planning discussions can create amongst the public, particularly people's antagonism to development, can be particularly marked. Issues with the council's other services can also give rise to controversy but often for a much more limited range and number of people. Whereas governments to the right of centre in the political spectrum might question the role of planning as a bureaucratic restriction on individual liberty or business activity, this is not necessarily true of most of the people who vote for them. Indeed, the wealthier the suburb was, the more its residents appeared to call for more, and stricter, planning. Far from wanting scope for more individualism, from what they say at public question time, and in their written comments in planning consultations, they want to see both their neighbours and property developers tightly constrained. However, this did not mean that they necessarily have an understanding of what planning is as a professional activity. Why should this be?

WHAT'S IN A NAME?

A large part of the problem lies in pinning down what planning is actually about. People tend to have a reasonably clear idea of what the content of the professions of law and medicine are all about, and also those more closely related to planning such as architecture and civil engineering, but not planning. The problem is often reflected in its name. At the start, we used the now rather antique term "town and country planning". This was the standard term in the first half of the 20th century. It was often shortened to "town planning" for convenience, but this was not meant to imply any exclusion of the rural dimension. In the second half of the 20th century, terms such as "urban and regional planning" and "environmental planning" became common but no new standard name used by everyone emerged. Shortening the name to "planning", as will often be done in this book, is common within the profession but can cause confusion with other types of planning when used outside of it. The problem with the name reflects another difficulty. The professional activities cover not only a very wide range of subject matter but also scale. At a given point in time, one planner might be dealing with aspects of regional economic policy while another with the protection of a particular tree.

Another problem in talking about what the word "planning" means is that there is a big difference between the grand idea and what actually happens in the planning office of a local council, or a firm of consultants, on a day-to-day basis. The planning of urban and rural areas requires thinking about where people will live, work, play, study, shop and how they will get about the place, and to plan this for long time periods. Unfortunately, a council planning department, generally speaking, has direct control only over the design and location of buildings and allocation of land to put new ones on. Nevertheless, while doing this, it needs to think about all the wider issues. Some components of urban areas, like parks, schools and roads, may be the responsibility of the local council but be under the control of different departments. Hospitals, universities, railways and buses will be under the control of private firms, or agencies of the central government, who may have much more real power than the local planning department. The central government will not only have its own policy on planning, which will control what a local council can and cannot do, but will also influence the planning of urban and rural areas through its policies on transport, health and education and many other matters. Planning as an activity is, therefore, part of a complex web stretching way beyond the planning office.

WHY IS PLANNING NEEDED?

Why do we need planning anyway? Why is it there? What is it for? What is striking is how universal it is. Planning systems exist in most countries across the world, or at least in their major urban areas. It is true that the presence of a planning system, i.e. legislation and officials to implement it, does not necessarily mean that the local system is effective or that it achieves much of value. If there is no political will, then there will still be little actual planning. For examples of non-plan outcomes, one has only to look at the larger cities in most third-world countries. Their problems of severe traffic congestion and low environmental standards are plain to see. Nevertheless, it is remarkable that cities in countries with widely differing cultures, political complexions and levels of development all feel the need to have a least a planning system, if not planning achievements. Like many other professions, it is not there because of the particular expert knowledge of its practitioners but because of the need to resolve particular issues as they affect people. Taking an analogy from medicine, even where there is no cure for a particular disease, the sick will still need to be cared for.

The essential feature common to all planning systems is the need to intervene in the process of urban and rural development to try to achieve an outcome that is more in line with the public interest. It may not be possible to achieve a perfect solution satisfying everybody, but there is a belief that an "optimal" solution is available. In other words, cities left to their own devices do not produce optimal outcomes. Some things may go right for some people some of the time, but there will be clear inefficiencies for the whole city for most of the time. Planning is based on the idea that there is a better solution. Planning also reflects a belief in a wider public interest.

People may ask how do you know what the public interest is. How do you recognise an optimal solution? Whose interests are being served and how are conflicts of interest resolved? The answer to these important questions is that this is what makes planning issues ultimately matters for political decision. Its professional practitioners may analyse the problems and indicate solutions, but the politicians have to make the final decisions. Planning is as much social and political as it is technical, if not more so.

Although "planning intervention" often means that a government agency called a "planning department" controls the activities of private developers, this is not always the case. Departments of government responsible for roads, schools, hospitals and other public services also carry out development, and their activities need to be coordinated through a planning system if it is to be effective. Although instances may be few, the public interest can also be served by intervention not just by government bodies but also by independent, properly constituted, trusts.

To illustrate the idea of an alternative, ideally optimal, outcome arising from intervention we can consider a simple example known to most holidaymakers, the development of beachfront hotels. In the beginning, a deserted stretch of tropical beach becomes to known to a few backpackers and then to the more adventurous tourists. Bungalows and small hotels are constructed, and more tourists arrive. More substantial hotels begin to be constructed along the shoreline.

Subsequently, a new airport is constructed nearby, and more and much larger hotels are built. Eventually, the whole shoreline is covered by very large hotels served by a new road. Over the years, the hotels become taller creating a visual barrier between the beach and the land behind. The original tourists complain that that what they came for has now been destroyed and they move on to find another, as yet unspoilt, beach. Those landowners that sell at the best time make a lot of money. The beachfront hotels do good business selling a view of the sea. Jobs are created for local and incoming people. However, it is not good news for all. Behind the wall of high-rise buildings, you cannot see the sea, and land values are very much lower than on the beachfront. The general standard of environment can be low with much motor traffic and a high level of noise. Where sewage, refuse and other pollutants are not properly removed, environmental degradation results. Where they are, the cost of doing so falls upon local taxpayers. In time, residential tower blocks are constructed which further reduce the visual quality but do not provide the same level of jobs as the hotels. Their occupants may not even be there for a large part of the year.

We can compare this with an actual example of alternative strategy that has actually been implemented and is economically successful. Back in 1978, the government of the Maldives took the advice of Danish consultants about how to develop the tourist potential of their numerous coral islands. The consultants advised that what the tourists came there for, coral reefs and pristine-secluded beaches, must be preserved at all costs and that hotel development should respect this requirement. As elsewhere in the world, the coral islands of the Maldives are very limited in their ability to absorb sewage, refuse and other pollutants. The advice was turned into policy and, as a result, what you do not get in the Maldives is hotels with an uninterrupted view of the beach. Some small islands have only one large hotel, some just a handful. They are all low rise and hidden from the beach behind bushes and trees that line the sand, as illustrated by Figure 0.1.

From the beach, you cannot see any hotels – it appears to be secluded. There are no beach or sea views from the hotel rooms, but that is the price that the tourists, and the hotel owners, have to pay. The number of hotels is restricted to the carrying capacity of the

Figure 0.1: Part of the Karumba resort in the Maldive Islands. Note the low buildings separated by trees from the beach. (Karumba, Maldives, www. kurumba.com)

environment. The coral reefs are maintained. However, the hotels still make money, and local jobs are still created. This can only happen because of the use of very strict planning controls and regulations that are focused on an outcome that is both visionary and achievable. It would have been possible to have alternative scenarios where more money was made and more jobs created, but there would also be economic losers and environmental costs that would be permanent. The final decision is a matter of values and, in consequence, a political one.

BIG AND SMALL STUFF

So, fundamentally, planning is about intervention in the process of development (as opposed to letting things be) in order to achieve a better outcome for everybody. In reality, this is a much bigger deal than this simple sentence conveys. It can result involvement in a wide range of social and economic issues. Getting an understanding of what "better" might mean, and for whom, is a complex social and political matter. Any intervention in the development process will have economic consequences. This is most prominent at the large scale where we are talking about how cities work. Unfortunately, planning has often been least successful at this scale. Planning systems exist throughout the world to address the major strategic issues of urban areas but are usually most effective at a small scale trying to fix local issues and disputes. We will take a close look at the small stuff later in this book, but to get a proper understanding of what planning is supposed to be all about, it is necessary to take a look at the big stuff first.

THE BIG STUFF – PLANNING GETS STARTED

PLANNING IS CONCEIVED AS A WAY OF CONFRONTING SOME BIG ISSUES

Since ancient times, governments and rulers have, from time to time, ordered the construction of whole new settlements – villages, towns and even great cities – and laid down rules for their design. While there are lessons that can be learnt from studying them, they were not what town planning is really about in the modern sense. Planning systems, as we know them today, have their origins in the industrial cities of the 19th century and the public reaction to the problems they caused. These cities brought great wealth to sections of the population and employment to most of the inhabitants. At their best, they created fine streets and buildings, roads and railways and were the source of the new technologies that made these feasible. However, as is well known, they had their downside – slum conditions for the really poor, overcrowding, disease and air and water pollution. Some of these could be solved by technology especially in the shape of sewerage and piped water. City councils could be empowered to regulate the design and layout of houses to ensure access to light and air. The issue, though, that was to give rise to the call for the planned city was that, for all their economic success, industrial cities possessed internal contradictions. In the long term, if left to their own devices, they did not function efficiently and deliver optimal outcomes for all their inhabitants. At, and around, the centre of the cities, land values were very high. This is where everyone wanted to be and where a lot of jobs were concentrated. Trying to fit everyone, and everything, in led to overcrowding and pollution. The invention of railways, buses and trams allowed the better-off to escape the central city. They could live further out and travel to work using this new public transport. On the outer edge of city, the land was cheaper, and they could afford bigger houses on larger plots. The suburb was born. Unfortunately, the poor could not afford to travel out and were forced live where land was expensive resulting in cramped living conditions and poor facilities. Their jobs were local because the city required their labour to function – bus drivers, cleaners, shop assistants, in addition to the factory workers. Employment was still local.

The first half of the 20th century brought changes, often for the better, but they did not resolve this basic dilemma regarding land values. On the contrary, the clamour in enlightened circles for planning to solve the problem increased. The use of electric power and motor vehicles brought about light industry that was less polluting and could be located out-of-town. Electric suburban and underground railways could spread out far into the surrounding countryside, as could new arterial roads. During the 1920s and 1930s, vast tracts of land were opened up for low-density suburban houses. Many could take advantage of these new homes, but critics considered these new buildings environmentally and visually intrusive, wasteful in their use of land and uncoordinated with local facilities. Most importantly, the older, poor-quality houses surrounding the centres of cities remained. Could not something be done? Could a planned city resolve these problems?

NATURE OF TOWNS AND CITIES

Before continuing, it would be a good idea to pause to clarify what goes to make up towns and cities and introduce some technical terms.

Urban areas exist primarily because of people's activities. Everyone needs somewhere to eat, sleep and relax. Most adults will be employed and will have somewhere where they work. Children need to go to school. All need to go to the shops, and the shops need to be supplied with goods. Factories also need to be supplied and to send out their products. People may need to go the doctor, dentist or seek hospital care. All will want to be entertained and some to engage in sports or other outdoor activities. The list could go on. All will need to travel between these activities by what are known as "modes" of transport: car, bus, train, walking or cycling. Goods need to be transported also, by lorry, van or train.

These activities need buildings. People live in dwellings – houses or flats. Their jobs are located not only in factories and offices but also in shops, hospitals, schools and many other places. Education takes place in schools, colleges and universities. Health service needs hospitals and local surgeries. The supply of goods needs warehouses. Again, the list could go on.

These buildings are linked together by other facilities that go to make what is technically known as "infrastructure". Travel takes place on roads, railways, cycleways and footpaths. There is also what is unseen: water supply, sewerage, gas and electricity.

All these buildings and infrastructure occupy land. This is where planning starts to get real as deciding which areas of land are to be used is something that it can control directly. Land is traded – it is bought and sold. Desirable land will have a high value. The buildings on the land also have a value and may be worth a lot of money. There is a market in land, and planning intervenes in this market.

All these activities, buildings and infrastructure should, in ideal circumstances, work together in a smooth and coordinated manner. The fact they do not always do this is why people often see a need for planning. However, planning is essentially preparation for the future, and the real need for it arises because things change over time. Change in urban areas is highly complex, mainly because change not only affects a lot of things but they all, in turn, have different components that can change at different rates. People may move house and move job, and children may move school, but these movements are not, in themselves, the main issue. The real challenge comes from the fact that people want more of them: more houses, more jobs, leading to more infrastructure. It is even more complex than that, because the nature of both employment and shopping changes over time as does the size and design of schools and hospitals. There is also the impact of new technology, particularly on transport and communications. If this were not enough, buildings and infrastructure can last for much longer than the activities they support so they have to be adaptable or be demolished. All in all, this adds up to quite a task.

THE BIG ISSUES

When it comes to finding solutions, it can be helpful to distinguish between the really big picture and smaller and more detailed issues. This definitely does not mean that the small stuff is less important – it certainly is not – nor that the big and small issues are not closely linked together – they certainly are. It is just that making the distinction can help to explain what is going on, given how complex it all is. In addition, when we talk of solutions, it is not just a matter of bricks and mortar but also of ways of managing urban areas over time, as they grow and change. By "managing" we are not just talking about law and procedures but how we handle both the big and small issues. What then are the big issues?

A DECENT HOME

People generally move to a city because they have, or want, a job there. In the 19th century, in spite of often squalid conditions, the industrial city still offered a better deal than that of the life of a farm labourer. The reason for the squalid conditions was that lots of people were all doing the same thing at the same time and in the same place. Doubtless, all would have liked a decent home, but they found, in practice, that nothing was available that they could afford and they had to put up with whatever they could get. The big challenge a planned city would face would be to provide well-designed homes in sufficient numbers for everybody and to keep on doing so.

A DECENT ENVIRONMENT

The competition for somewhere to live and work in urban areas not only created pollution, not just from factories but also from vehicles (horses then, petrol now) together with household sewage and other waste, all contributing to the squalid conditions. The big challenge for a planned city would be how to bring about a decent, healthy and liveable environment as well as provide transport, open space for recreation and places for education and entertainment, and to maintain all this over time.

LAND VALUES – THE CORE ISSUE

At the core of dilemma was, and has always been, the issue of land values. It is where the contradictions of the inner city lay and, consequently, the sub-standard living conditions. What the proponents of planning also drew attention to was the way that land values increased over time as urban areas expanded. Imagine you owned farmland fairly near to a city. As that edge of the urban area grew out towards it, its value went up. Once the city surrounded your land it became very valuable indeed. However, you had done nothing yourself to bring about the increase in value. You had not made anything, or provided any service, to cause it. It was what became known as an "unearned increment", and the technical name for it was "betterment". Could not this increase in value be captured for the public good? Could not some system be devised to resolve the contradictions in land values at the heart of the problem of the industrial city?

THE FIRST SOLUTIONS
THE GARDEN CITY

It is here that we come to what could be seen as the first great step forward in the development of planning as we know it today, Ebenezer Howard's "Garden City". It is important not just because of the publication of his ideas, remarkable as they were, at the turn of the 19th and 20th centuries, but because Howard and his associates carried their ideas into bricks and mortar by building the world's first two garden cities, Letchworth and Welwyn, in England. They can still be seen today, and visitors can take a look at them themselves and make their own judgements about them. Howard's basic idea was that publicly minded citizens could get together to form a legal trust, which would buy up a large area of land in a rural location at a low price. They would seek investors to put money in order to finance the construction, by the trust, of a new town on this land. New residents would rent from, and be shareholders in, the trust. As the town grew, the value of the land, and other assets owned by the trust, would rise. This increase in wealth, the betterment, would then be shared by the residents. It would also be used to repay the original investors and finance the further growth of the town. It would be neither a completely public nor an entirely private development – something in-between. The built form would be characteristic of neither the industrial city nor the countryside but would be something that incorporated the best of both of them, while having none of their disadvantages, in other words a "garden city".

Letchworth was built from 1903 onwards in a country cottage style, with ample trees and green spaces, as illustrated in Figure 1.1. It had its own railway station, although on a local line. Although some factories and shops came along, their number was below expectations. The second attempt was to prove more successful in this regard. Howard bought more land at Welwyn, around a railway station on the main line, and the second garden city was built there from 1919 onwards. From fairly early on, factories were built on one side of the

Figure 1.1: Street view in Letchworth Garden City, showing terraced houses with trees and lawns. Although terraces are common in Letchworth, there is a wide range of house types in the Garden City, including some fairly large detached houses. (Tony Hall)

Figure 1.2: Street view in Welwyn Garden City showing terraced houses with trees and lawns. Although the type of house is similar to that in Letchworth as shown in Figure 1.1, note the use of a neo-classical style. There is a wide range of other house types in Welwyn, including streets of fairly large detached houses. (Tony Hall)

line and a shopping centre with a department store on the other. The architectural style was neo-classical rather than "country cottage" but was still a house-and-garden form as can be seen in Figure 1.2.

A problem with the name "garden city" is that it often conjures up a "country cottage" picture in the mind and can obscure the wider principles that garden cities were meant to be all about. A house-and-garden layout with plenty of public open space and trees was, indeed, an important part of the plan but it did not need to be "country cottage" in style. What was just as important was how to deliver both houses and infrastructure in the right numbers, in the right place and in an affordable manner.

NEW LAWS FOR PLANNING AND HOUSING

In Britain, the period of the establishment of the first garden cities at the beginning of the 20th century also saw the first planning legislation, the 1909 Town and Country Planning Act. A second act followed in 1932. However, neither of these established a comprehensive planning system. All they did was to empower local councils to adopt planning schemes for specific localities. A nationwide system had to wait until after the end of the Second World War. 1919 saw the first legislation to introduce "council housing", houses built by local councils on land they had purchased for subsidised rent to lower income households. The government published guidance on how they were to be designed that reflected the outward "house and garden" form of the garden cities, as can be seen in the example shown in Figure 1.3.

However, to get cheap land to build on meant locating large, uniform estates on the edge of existing urban areas, often some distance from main centres of shopping and entertainment.

The 1930s saw extensive, and almost unregulated, suburban expansion of towns and cities through the construction of privately built estates of family houses giving rise to public complaints about

Figure 1.3: Council houses in Morden, London, built in the 1930s. Note the use of terraced houses with front gardens, together with an avenue of trees and lawns. (Tony Hall)

urban "sprawl". Public debate in progressive circles calling for a planning system that would address wider social and economic issues increased as a result. In the 1940s, the experience of wartime conditions further bolstered the desire to build again in a new way that would be beneficial to society as a whole. In addition, the war effort showed how governments could make a big difference by organising public enterprise on a hitherto unprecedented scale.

The history of planning in Britain reached a remarkable threshold with the passage of the 1946 New Towns Act and 1947 Town and Country Planning Act. The 1947 Act nationalised the right to develop land which was now exercised by the state. Local County and County Borough Councils (as they were then) were to control development in accordance with local development plans. These plans required the approval of the central government and were to be revised every five years. The central government set up a Ministry of Town and Country Planning to oversee the process. An essential feature of the new act was that the "betterment", i.e. the increase in land value resulting from the granting of permission to develop, was to be taxed at 100%. This proportion has been the subject of debate ever since, but the idea was to remove issues of land value from the planning process altogether. The criticism that has been levelled at it was that it removed the incentive to develop land. In the event, this provision for the taxation betterment was repealed in 1951 by the government of the day, although all powers to make development plans, and to control of development, carried on without it.

The requirement to keep development plans up-to-date, also proved problematic, an issue has continued to the present day. The plans took councils a long time to prepare, and the central government took even longer to approve them. When it came to revising the plans, the time scale slipped alarmingly to the extent that a five-year rolling programme became totally unrealistic. However, the important point was that these controversies and shortcomings did not result in the other major features of the act, aside from the taxation of betterment, being repealed, much less the idea of a comprehensive system being abandoned. Although the way the system operated would be revised many times, through a succession of further acts, the vesting of the right to develop land in the state has remained. This has also remained a fundamental characteristic of planning systems in many other countries. Development plans have changed in their design and format, but they have remained a basic feature, as has the desire, if not always the practice, that they should be kept up-to-date. Powers to control the details of development, such as the design and location of buildings, have also remained ever since and have sometimes appeared to become the predominant activity of local planning authorities. However, the problem about the repeal of the taxation of betterment was that it struck at the very notion of what town and country planning had originally been seen to be all about, particularly about how it sought to finance infrastructure and public housing, and we will need to return to these matters in the next chapter.

NEW TOWNS

The 1946 New Towns Act (still on the statute book at the time of writing) empowered the government to acquire land at existing use value within an area of land designated for a new town. In other words, it would publish a map showing the boundary of the land required for the proposed town and would have the power to buy most of the land at agricultural prices. Infrastructure (essentially the roads, schools, parks and other main services) and housing would be built using government loans and repaid over time from receipts and other income. The big difference from Howard's "Garden City" idea was principally that these activities were to be carried out by the state and managed by unelected, and temporary, development corporations, although with the intention (never carried out) that the assets would be transferred to local councils in the fullness of time. Although this last point did not happen, what did happen was that, in the late 1940s, eight new towns were designated in a ring around London, two in Northeast England and two in Scotland. What is more, and of great significance, is that all of them repaid their loans and, 30 years later, showed a substantial surplus in their accounts. What is remarkable is that this programme of construction was carried out when the national economy was still in a parlous state, recovering from exertions of the Second World War. Over and above the financial success, the advantage of the New Town idea was that they could be properly designed from the outset. Town centres with all the shops, as illustrated in Figure 1.4, and all necessary infrastructure could be provided at every stage.

Figure 1.4: The central square of Stevenage New Town, built in the 1950s. The style is fresh and modern but of human scale. (Tony Hall)

A range of housing could be provided to meet the requirements of all income levels and family sizes or, at very least, these could be achieved to a far greater extent than with piecemeal public and private development. The results are on the ground for readers to judge. The disadvantages of new towns were mainly political. Most of the cost and nearly all of the local opposition from existing residents was up front and concentrated. On the other hand, with incremental and dispersed development, opposition may be more fragmented (albeit still intense), and it is easier to get away with failing to provide all of the infrastructure as, and when, it is needed. Later on, it was also seen as government controlling the whole development process (as opposed to just planning it) with a burden (although temporary) on public borrowing. Although New Towns continued to be designated during the 1950s and 1960s, the last was in 1970. In total, 28 were built housing, at the time of writing, 2–3 million people.

As we have just noted, an important principle of Howard's Garden City was that infrastructure, public facilities and other major landholdings should remain in communal ownership. The government would pay for them to be constructed by the development corporation. When, eventually, the development corporation was wound up, the original idea was that these assets would pass to the local council. However, this was not to be. During the 1950s, the government made the political decision to transfer them instead to a central government body, the Commission for New Towns. Another political decision was made during the 1980s to wind up the Commission for New Towns and sell off its assets. Not only is it important to note that during the first half of the 20th century the public or local council ownership of infrastructure and other assets was part of what planning was believed to be all about, but there is still relevance here for current practice. The next chapter will discuss how infrastructure is to be paid for in relation to new development. The question that should also arise is who subsequently owns this infrastructure and how does the public at large benefit from this ownership?

Particular mention must be made of Milton Keynes which was intended not so much as a new town as a "new city". It was one of the last clutch of new towns designated around 1964–67. It was not only on a larger scale than the post-war new towns but was a response to different pressures. Whereas the first new towns were intended to accommodate people moving out from London or other major cities (so called "overspill") Milton Keynes was intended to be one of several new cities that would be need to accommodate what was then predicted be a substantial increase in population, particularly in South-east England. Its layout reflected what had, at the time, become two prevailing views. Firstly, new cities must reflect the predominant use of the car. Secondly, they should be able to cope with the continuous expansion over a long time period. (The first new towns were seen as growing to a planned fixed size and remaining like that.) It was, therefore, designed around a grid of major roads set 1-km intervals, as shown in Figure 1.5.

According to opinion polls, as a planned car-based city, this layout is, apparently, popular with its car-owning residents. Unfortunately, it makes it difficult for the efficient operation of bus services. Although some other late new towns, such as Cumbernauld in Scotland, were built with full-scale facilities for motor vehicles,

Figure 1.5: An aerial view of part of the new city Milton Keynes, built from the 1970s onwards. Note how the main roads are arranged in the form of a rectangular grid (Ian Bracegirdle)

including what were, effectively, urban motorways, Milton Keynes was the only one with a complete grid form. However, this was, in retrospect, the high point of building around car-use, and the trend since then has been away from designing car-based cities. Nevertheless, Milton Keynes remains important for current practice as it is still being expanded and even, in parts, re-built, a process that may continue for the foreseeable future.

Free-standing new towns were not the only way that central government legislation was used to cope with urban expansion and relocation of population. From the early 1950s onwards, several small towns particularly in South-east England were selected for expansion to several times their original size. The idea was that those selected might be seen as not having previously grown to their full size, were in an area of increasing prosperity and housing demand, had an existing feeling of identity and character and, hopefully under-used facilities that might be taken advantage of. In the later 1960s, about the time Milton Keynes was being designated, this idea moved up a gear to the designation of "expanded cities", Peterborough,

Northampton and Warrington, existing cities that, although well connected by road rail, had never reached what was thought to be their full potential.

This period of investment in new towns and cities did not last. By the late 1970s, government policy had turned against designating any more of them. Although it had always been present, the intense opposition to them from existing residents began to be seen as an insuperable obstacle. For this, and also, for cost-saving reasons, especially avoiding expenditure on new infrastructure and other facilities, emphasis was now placed on development on derelict or underused land within existing urban areas, so-called "brownfield sites", or by adding extensions bit-by-bit to existing towns. This was to continue in a strict form until at least the 2000s and, in essence, to the present day. Why the present situation could not be considered the "strict form" is that governments are now prepared to encourage a limited number of free-standing new settlements, effectively, small towns or large villages. These may be given the label "eco" or "garden", but whether or not this is appropriate may be judged from whether they fit the brief planning history set out above. Although the design of their houses was always important, the real meaning of the "garden city", and also the "new towns", lay in how financial and environmental benefit for the residents was both achieved and preserved.

2

THE FIRST BIG ISSUES – HOUSES
AND INFRASTRUCTURE

We have seen, in the previous chapter, how town and country planning was originally conceived as a way of dealing with land values in a way that would make it much easier to provide everyone with a decent home within reach of jobs, schools, health facilities, parks and other opportunities for recreation. This would apply just as much in rural as urban areas. Different methods for achieving this, garden cities, new towns and laws providing for the taxation of betterment had not only been thought up but actually carried out in practice. Unfortunately, they have not, in general, been continued with. To some, this shows a failure of planning. On the other hand, there are some alternative, although not as comprehensive, ways of trying to make progress without direct control of land values. There are also other things that planning systems have ended up doing, often quite successfully, at medium and small scales. In this chapter, we will take a look at what planning can still do for housing, jobs and infrastructure at the large scale. The smaller-scale issues will be described in later chapters.

PROVIDING AFFORDABLE HOUSING

Central to the story so far has been the contradiction at the heart of the city – how can low-income people afford to live near their jobs in anything like a decent manner? To a large extent, this is a separate area of public policy, housing policy and a concern of another set of professionals, housing managers. However, it is also clearly bound up with the concerns of town planning. If you cannot tax betterment or acquire land at existing use value, what can you do? Several European countries, (Germany and Denmark come to mind) but not Britain, have attempted to solve the problem by giving powers to government or quasi-government public bodies to acquire land at below market value in order to provide affordable housing. There are a number of different types of scheme, but the evidence is that they are reasonably successful in meeting the demand for housing. This is not the same as building a new town, as it is only for housing schemes and not always for infrastructure and jobs, but for small-scale estates it does appear to be the next best thing.

In Britain, from the 1920s to the 1970s, the policy was to allow local councils to buy up land on which they built, and managed, housing that they let at subsidised rents. This became known as "council housing" but, without powers to buy land at near existing use value, it could not get around the central dilemma. Very large numbers of often soundly built and laid out estates of houses and gardens were built during the 1930s and 1950s. Unfortunately, to find large areas of land which was fairly cheap at market prices, councils had to build on the edge of cities. Families, usually at that time without car, were placed a long way from amenities, and often employment as well, and the estates represented huge concentrations of people of the same social and economic backgrounds all in one place.

The alternative was to build at a very high density in an around the centres of cities. In the event, this produced even more, and even more severe, problems. High density meant very high blocks of flats which were very expensive both to build and to maintain and, therefore, to live in. Small households on higher incomes can make a success of them because they can afford the substantial extra cost of lifts, gardening, cleaning of common areas, reception, maintenance and security staff. However, during the 1960s, it was implemented on a large scale as a means of housing low-income families on subsided rents in most European countries, North America and even in parts of Australia. An economic boom during the late 1950s had provided the money to demolish the sub-standard houses around the centres of cities and replace it with these high-rise flats, as illustrated by the example in Figure 2.1.

Figure 2.1: High-rise council flats at Castle Vale, Birmingham, built in the 1960s. (Now demolished and replaced largely by two-storey houses.) (Tony Hall)

Unfortunately, for a local council with a limited budget to house low-income households in this way did not add up. They would not have been able to afford to construct them in the first place had a central government subsidy not been available. Eventually, the costs of maintenance, heating and security began to present almost insuperable challenges. In addition, such accommodation was at least restricting, and at worst totally unsuitable, for families with children. In many cases, the results were catastrophic, and most (although not all) of the high-rise blocks built for subsidised housing from this period has now been demolished.

From the 1980s onwards, the construction of much, often most, affordable housing was provided by a tax on development rather than government expenditure, although some government money was still available for direct building by housing associations. Developers had to prove at least 20%–25% of dwellings within their schemes as affordable, in some locations much more. The housing stock was increasingly managed by not-for-profit housing trusts. There is one obvious limitation to this policy. It provides the affordable housing only when and where it is profitable to build dwellings for owner occupation, and where local planning policy allows them to be built, which may not necessarily when, and where, there is the need for it.

PROVIDING ENOUGH HOUSES

Housing policy is not just about providing enough affordable housing in the right place for people on low incomes. It is also about providing the much larger number of dwellings for owner-occupiers and for letting at market rents. There is also an affordability aspect for owner-occupiers. Young people seeking to buy their own home for the first time will need to be able to afford to enter the market. If prices are too high for them, there will be few first-time buyers. A general inflation in house prices may be seen as good news by those already owning, but it is bad news not just for the first-time buyers but also for governments, who fear the destabilising effects on the economy, particularly the diversion of money into unproductive investment. Land prices can go down as well as up, and money invested in land does not, of itself, produce more goods and services.

House price rises are driven by two broad components – availability of credit and the supply and demand for land and houses. A large part of the supply and demand side is, as estate agents always emphasise, location. People compete to live in certain locations that they see as desirable while shunning less desirable ones, and location is what planning is all about. Supply is largely a question of providing enough dwellings in the right places. Demand is affected by the size of the population as a whole and the proportions of it wanting to live in particular areas. However, it is not as simple as just the total number of people. The demand for dwellings depends on how people arrange themselves into families and households. The number of households may go up even when the size of the population is constant. More marriages may break up leading the couple to separate; young people may leave home earlier; there has been for many decades an increasing disinclination to share houses with others, especially older relatives and so on. Contemporary social trends have tended exacerbate all these factors. From the purely technical point of view, it is possible to calculate the changes in population size and structure and the numbers of households formed and make predictions that are reasonably sound. It is also possible to have a stab at estimating migration flows around the country, not just in terms of desirable areas but also in how they may be following the movement of jobs. From a professional point of view, planners can have a very good go at estimating likely demand both nationally and locally. The planning problem is really one of supply.

It is not in a developer's interest for the price of land and buildings to fall too steeply or suddenly. Housebuilders tend to regulate the supply in order to maintain a steady selling price. The extent to which they do this is, and whether this has a large-scale effect on the supply of housing nationally, is very controversial. Developers may claim that they need more land with planning permission for housing, but their critics may argue that there is ample land to build on but the housebuilders are not building on all of what they have. One fact is clear. The highest building rate for houses in Britain was in the 1950s and 1960s, when it was largely being carried out by local councils and was far in excess of the rate of building in more recent decades which has been predominantly by the private sector.

However, a major problem on the supply side is that the general public does not see the situation as the planning profession or central government see it. The general public are not, in general, aware of the estimates of demand for more houses and the arguments for meeting this demand. They would not necessarily agree with them if they did. Local councillors do not generally come across strong local pressure for more houses to be built. (If they were able to find some, it would make their task very much easier.) On the contrary, people oppose additional development in general and more houses in particular. This may not just be because of any impact on their own house or immediate locality, nor about "losing countryside", although they would most certainly object to these, but because of concern about the general increase in the size of cities towns and villages bringing with it more traffic, more crowding and more competition for amenities. Owner-occupiers welcome the increase house prices, as they see it as making them wealthier. Even those who might benefit from lower house prices do not necessarily see more houses as a solution. What they want is access to the existing supply so that they can rent or buy. However, if they are prospective first-time buyers, then they would want what they bought to go up in value. What all welcome is the presence of a planning system as their protection from new development.

This impasse lies at the heart of much of the failure of planning to achieve its goals at the large scale. It makes it very difficult to get proposals approved at the local level. They are approved because the central government ensures, through its control of planning policy and through the mechanism of planning appeals, that local feelings cannot frustrate development in the long term. However, it makes the whole issue of meeting the demand for housing an uphill struggle and, in recent decades, this demand, both nationally and locally, has never been met. If there were local pressure for more houses from the public at large, then the whole process would be transformed.

Surely, some readers may say, there is a problem finding the land for all these new houses. Looked at in aggregate across the country, there is no problem as the actual area taken up by new housing schemes is very small compared to the quantity of undeveloped land available. However, this does not take into account the competition for the best locations. There is a shortage of land where everyone wants to be, and this creates the high land values with which our story started and to which it keeps returning. This leads on to the issue of residential density – the number of dwellings on a given area of land. As land values rise, it becomes profitable for developers to buy up existing houses and gardens and replace them with blocks of flats. This process will also be resisted by local residents as it changes the character of their local area where they had always lived or had chosen to live. As will be discussed later in this book, a lot can depend on how this housing designed. It can be done well or badly. Unfortunately, though, the overall local political problem of public opposition to development will always be there.

PAYING FOR INFRASTRUCTURE

Let us now consider infrastructure. New urban areas need roads, water supply, sewerage, energy supplies, schools, hospitals, parks and so on. Should these all be paid for, and managed thereafter, directly out of taxes, as is commonly the case for roads and schools? In an unplanned situation, new development would normally be led by the private sector, and this tends to leave the public sector endeavouring to catch up after the event. How then to ensure that all necessary infrastructure is provided at the right time and in the right quantity? Is this not what proper planning should be all about? How can private development not impose an undue burden on the taxpayer? If planning were infrastructure-led, then development would be allowed only when the taxpayer could afford the facilities to support it. However, this would be unlikely to meet the demand for houses and jobs in a timely manner and failure to do this would cause more political problems.

In the late 1940s, all these arguments led to the creation of a planning system that included the taxation of betterment and planned new towns. As we have seen, taxation of betterment did not last beyond the early 1950s and, by the late 1970s, new towns were also out of favour. Governments were, nevertheless, still concerned about having to find all the money needed for infrastructure up front and moves began to make private developments pay at least a large part of their costs. The law was changed to permit planning permission to be conditional upon an agreement being signed between the developer and the local council that would commit the developer to paying for an agreed list of necessary items of infrastructure. Note that it is the "development" not the "developer" that ultimately pays – the developer is only a transitory part of the process. In theory at least, the costs should come from a reduction in the price paid for the land, i.e. the landowner's unearned increment. Development can only go ahead if it can make a profit. The income from the scheme must exceed the combined costs of the land and the costs of building upon it. If infrastructure costs have to be paid for by the development, then the developer cannot afford to offer so much for the land. If all these costs are all known in advance, then land prices should go down. Unfortunately, it may not always work out so neatly in practice, but at least that is the theory. The advantage of negotiated agreements is that they can be tailored to the particular requirements large schemes. The disadvantages are that they are subject to vagaries and uncertainties of negotiation and are practical only for very large developments. They do not take into account the cumulative demand for facilities arising from the very large number of small proposals that are being approved all the time. At the time of writing, an alternative approach was being phased in whereby a standard proportional infrastructure charge is levied on all developments. While this deals with the issue of the aggregate demand from small proposals, a problem that arises is that the income from them may not necessarily come in when the council is in a position to spend it. It depends on having a properly planned programme for infrastructure provision.

3

MORE BIG ISSUES – EMPLOYMENT AND THE REGIONS

PLANNING FOR CHANGING EMPLOYMENT

Taking account of jobs is one of the biggest challenges that planning faces. Where will people work, in what capacity and with what land requirements? Planners are expected to allocate land on which people will work. New towns and new suburbs are expected to contain jobs for the people who live there. Moreover, there is a particular "value" or "goal" that has been associated with planning from the beginning: people should live near to where they work. Professionally, this has often been seen as a "good thing".

Here we come up against the gap between the wider issues that "planning" is concerned with and what actually can be done in the "planning office". Planning can allocate land, but it has difficulty in controlling what happens on this land afterwards. Land for housing is relatively straightforward here. You can normally guarantee that houses will arrive on the land allocated, and it is likely to stay that way for a very long time. On the other hand, if land is allocated for jobs, how do you make sure the jobs come there and, if they do, keep them there? Another problem is that people are not only employed in factories and offices but also in shops, schools, hospitals and many other services. Many offices and other services may share land not only with each other but also with housing – what is called "mixed uses". Overlaying all this is the problem that the very nature of the jobs that people work at keeps changing. Roads and buildings can be there for at least 50 years and probably many centuries. On the other hand, the nature and location of employment can change dramatically over the time periods that planning deals with: 20, 10, even 5, years let alone the length of time over which buildings last.

By way of illustration, and at the risk of over simplification, the wider pattern of the changes in western advanced economies could be seen as follows. The 19th century industrial city was usually based on manufacturing industry as its economic driver. Heavy industry such as iron and steel might be located near water and coal supplies. They were in, or near to, city centres and served by steam railways. Cities might commonly have textile mills and light manufacturing also located within them. Growth in the 20th century saw estates for light industry powered by electricity, served by motor vehicles and located on the edge of towns and cities. In both periods, "real jobs" were for "men" and involved "making things" in "factories" on "industrial estates', or so it was commonly perceived. However, providing services had always been there in parallel with manufacturing. Since the 19th century, people have been required to drive trains and buses, to serve in shops and to construct, maintain and clean buildings. There have always been people providing financial, legal and health services, with significant concentrations of these in the centres of larger cities.

During the latter part of the 20th century, employment in both heavy and light industry declined, both through the increased use of automation and because a lot of it transferred to third world countries, though not the extent that it disappeared completely. This left employment in services as the mainstay. The 1960s and 1970s saw a rapid increase in office workers housed in office towers in cities. The end of the 20th century saw a decline in the size of large corporate headquarters, largely because of advances in IT, but the need for some significant office space, particularly in major financial centres, did not go away. What, however, is often overlooked is that, outside of financial and legal services and the management of large businesses, there are other concentrations of service employment to be found in all towns and cities. Health and education are important sources of employment. Large university and hospital complexes do not just employ academics, doctors and nurses but people in a range of jobs at all income levels. However, one of the largest sources of jobs is retailing. Shops are labour-intensive, and they do not just employ shop assistants. Moreover, shops themselves have also been subject to rapid change. Whereas local suburban centres, high streets and city centre shopping remain and can be successful, the latter part of the 20th century and early 21st century saw the growth of large stores and shopping malls located on the edge of, or outside of, urban areas, of ever-increasing scale. To say all this is not necessarily to make any judgements about whether this is a "good thing", at least at this stage, but just to show the scale of the challenges that planners face. Subsequently, the increasing scale of internet shopping had a substantial impact on all these trends.

As we have said, the planning process can control only the location and quantity of land and access to it by roads and railways. It does not control the ever-changing economic forces. Those that seek to control them have not had a good record of forecasting the changes. Those that advise them, such as estate agents and property consultants, may examine recent trends and may not have a sound way of forecasting future changes. Planners may be left having to make their own informed guesses, but they also face an additional problem. The political pressures may be to resist the changes or pretend that they are not happening. The case of the decline of manufacturing and heavy industry is a particular case in point. The idea that the "real jobs" are on industrial estates, and jobs in services, such as those in shops and hospitals, are not "real jobs" dies very hard.

It is not all doom and gloom though. Because of where they stand, planners, if they are imaginative, can play a very important role to play. As factories, office blocks, schools and shopping centres change, land may be released for other purposes. The construction of new factories offers not just the opportunity for new design but also for planners to control it. Outmoded and unused factories can be an important source of new land for housing, but there can be no going back to other uses once it has been released for this purpose. This leads in to the very important subject of local economic regeneration, which is discussed in more detail in Chapter 6.

To continue with the wider picture, there are other employment issues that planners have to wrestle with that need to be discussed. As mentioned at the beginning of this chapter, there has always been an understanding amongst planners that people should live near where they work and that this should be borne in mind in the design of new urban areas. This was originally for social and quality of life reasons – the time spent travelling could be spent in more productive and enjoyable ways. These arguments have been reinforced by subsequent concerns about sustainability. If the need to travel could be reduced, then so could the use of energy. Unfortunately, it does not seem to be how people have actually behaved when given a choice and left to make their own decisions. People appear to allocate a fixed amount of time to travelling. If they can travel faster, they travel farther. They give priority to a cheaper house price, or to living in a semi-rural area, over time taken in getting to work. People may live in one area but choose to work a long way away, and this is outside the planners' control. Nevertheless, a "dormitory suburb" is still considered a "bad thing", meaning that there should always be some local employment. Certainly, if there were none at all it would rule out the possibility of anyone living near to where they work, even if they wanted to. There is still the question of the size and nature of even a small amount of local employment. For example, do local shops count as employment? Are they "real jobs"?

There is also the important, and controversial, issue of jobs in the countryside. The 20th century saw a dramatic decline in jobs in agriculture. However, it still exists, and wages are still comparatively low. On the other hand, there has been an increase in tourism and leisure jobs, such as bed and breakfast accommodation, "horseyculture" and so on. Again, not great numbers or high incomes for most employees, but, nevertheless, they can be important for those still employed. For those working in the countryside, they may see a decline in the amount of services, shops, schools, health facilities and public transport and may not have the spare cash to move to where these can now be found. Should, then, more employment be encouraged in the countryside? Would these be newly created jobs or would allocating land for them just mean that existing firms move out of urban areas bringing in their employees with them, thus creating reverse car-based commuting? It can be an attractive prospect for some businesses, such as car repairers, but may not necessarily bring benefits overall. The reason for making these points is to draw attention to the dilemmas that planning policy has to confront and for which there may be no easy answers. They also take us on to wider countryside issues, discussed in the next chapter, of which employment is just one important part.

REGIONAL ISSUES – THE REALLY BIG SCALE

Living near to where you work is one thing, but changes in the nature and location of work, as already discussed, can take place over a very wide canvas, often amounting to large parts of countries, usually referred to as "regions". Regions may have a cultural or linguistic basis, Wales being a clear example in the British context, but for most planning purposes we are talking about economic regions. For the Welsh example, most of South Wales is quite different to most of North Wales in terms of its economic history. There are at least two different economic regions.

What we find worldwide is that economic regions can cross not just cultural but national boundaries. The growth of heavy industry based on coal and iron in the 19th century occurred not just in specific regions of countries but also in specific regions of continents, as in the case of Europe and North America. These substantial areas, centred on large cities, declined in their prosperity during the second half of the 20th century. In the first half of the 20th century, the growth of light industry powered by electricity was not necessarily in the same parts of countries and continents. These industries too have been subject to decline in developed countries towards the end of the 20th century. The early 21st century saw the growth of high-tech "silicon valleys", regions where the economy has been driven by new types of technological innovation. By regions in a planning sense, we mean, therefore, areas of similar economic activity. They may be hundreds of kilometres wide incorporating a range of cities of varying sizes.

What has all this to do with planning? Well, these economic trends affect where people want to live. Housing demand follows the location of economic growth (aside from people retiring to desirable locations). Not only will economic growth change between, and within, regions but journeys to work will also occur, and change, at a regional scale. Transport improvements can change the pattern of housing demand. Motorways and faster trains can provide shorter journey times enabling people to live further from their work, some-time over a 100 km radius, effectively commuting at a regional scale.

How does all this affect the practice of planning? What happens in the planning office? Although most professional planning activity may take place at a fairly local scale, it cannot escape the changes at a regional scale, particularly when it comes to housing and em-ployment. A whole number of planning decisions need to be made at the regional scale, whether or not there are planning authorities whose boundaries correspond to those of the economic regions. In the absence of regional authorities, they may be made by the central government or its agencies. At the regional scale, what action can planners take, though, that is distinct from those of national gov-ernments? The first and most obvious point is that trends must be analysed, understood and predicted. Not necessarily an easy matter, but an important one because of its effect on particular locations at a smaller scale. What, though, can actually be done to change and influence these economic and social trends at a regional scale? Is changing them not what planning is supposed to be all about? The argument one way is that to change regional trends is a daunt-ing challenge for national governments and planning activities may appear puny when compared to what governments attempt to do. The argument the other way is that a certain number of strategic decisions on the location of roads, railways and airports need to be made, and these are planning decisions. Planning is necessary in a core sense, but the political context in which it operates means that success may be elusive.

The history of planning practice at the regional level in the UK has, unfortunately, been a very uneven one. From very little in the 1950s, a high point was reached in the late 1960s, driven in large part by concern about the consequences of a significantly increased birth rate. The birth rate eventually went down again but, at the time, the question was where to put the increase in the population. Substantial regional studies, notably the South-east Study of 1964 and South-east Strategy of 1967, supplemented by a number of sub-regional studies centred on selected major cities. However, these good times were not to last. During the 1970s, both the birth rate and economic growth declined and with them the pressure for planning substan-tial new towns and cities and transport links at the regional scale.

Planning for regions of economic decline was still carried out in the hope of doing something to regenerate them, but finding successful remedies proved difficult in practice. Subsequently, emphasis on regional planning has come and gone with governments of different complexions, eventually leading to the situation in England at the time of writing where there is, effectively, none at all.

To understand the whys and wherefores of this changing situation, it is helpful to make a distinction between:

- regional trends;
- regional planning;
- regional administration;
- regional government.

We have already discussed the first two, the inevitability of regional trends and how they need to be taken account of in planning and how they should, ideally, be expressed in regional plans. For the second two, we can note that many Western European countries, such as France, Germany, Italy and Spain, have regional governments with their own legal powers and finances and their own administrative set up. A wide range of decisions, including planning are taken at the regional level. In the UK, the central government has always been all-powerful and apart from the special case of Northern Ireland, regional government was unknown before the late 1990s when devolved governments were established in Scotland and Wales. Before then, from the 1960s onwards, there were regional administrations, but these civil servants were responsible to the government in Westminster. Regional administrations continued within England until 2011. In Scotland and Wales, as with regions of other European countries, how well they carry out regional planning may vary over time, and from region to region, but they all have the power to adopt and enforce regional plans and policies at any time. In contrast, the situation in England is that local councils now have to do their best individually, and sometime collectively, to take account the effect of the consequences of regional trends themselves.

MORE BIG ISSUES – HEALTH, ENVIRONMENT AND THE COUNTRYSIDE

The reader should not need to be told afresh here about the concerns expressed for the Earth's environment, about the pressures upon it and the effects of climate change. The question here is how these important worldwide issues interact with planning functions, even down to quite a local level. Not just readers, but many other people and national governments, may say "what is this all to with what happens in a planning office"?

From time to time, governments can, and do, try to say that these issues are not part of the compass of planning but the job of national departments and agencies or private firms. For example, in Britain, while there was a period in the 1970s when the central government saw planning as belonging within a coordinated environmental ministry along with transport and housing, there have been many other periods when it has come under housing, without explicit connections to transport, jobs, heritage and the natural environment which were the preserve of other ministries. The same sort of thing can be found in other countries. However, it does not prevent the development of land being affected by, and having an effect on, large-scale environmental, social and economic trends, some of which may, in some cases, transcend national boundaries. Even if one attempts to define planning very narrowly as control over the development of land, it soon becomes impossible, in practice, to separate it out from wider environmental issues. It is important, therefore, to take a look at how environmental concerns and planning functions interact.

THE HEALTHY CITY

At the time of writing, there has been a resurgence of interest in the idea that one of the aims of planning is to create urban and rural areas that encourage and facilitate a healthy population. During the late 19th century and early 20th century, health issues were very much behind the pursuit of safe sewage disposal, a clean water supply and the removal of air pollution. By the late 20th century, these goals had been largely achieved, and health issues were seen more in terms of the treatment of disease, and separate matters from the design of towns and cities.

Nevertheless, in the early 21st century, there was the growing realisation that, given the achievements in sanitation and medicine, the pursuit of health was now much more a matter of lifestyle. Not only was diet important, but also exercise, for stimulating cardio-vascular health and weight loss. The use of cars for nearly all journeys worked against such healthy activities. The quantity of exercise can be encouraged or discouraged by the design of urban areas. Parks, sports facilities and other open spaces, have always been provided in towns and cities, but it is not just a matter of how easy it is to get to them but that exercise could be encouraged by their very design and layout, in other words it should be "built in". The design of urban areas should not just make it easier to get about without a car but also make it pleasurable and safe to walk and cycle. How this can be done is discussed further in Chapters 5 and 6.

Air pollution is another vital matter. Historically from the 19th century to the middle of the 20th century, it was smoke from home fires and industrial processes that was the main problem. This has now been largely solved, apart from certain industries in specific locations, but has been replaced by the pollution caused by the exhaust of motor vehicles. The layout of urban areas brings these vehicles into direct contact with pedestrians and people living nearby, and their design, therefore, bears directly upon this issue. As with the promotion walking and cycling, it comes within the subject of transport design issues, which are also discussed in the following chapters.

THE IMPACT OF THE CITY ON THE COUNTRYSIDE

Many readers, and the public at large, may say that a healthy city is all very well but what of its environmental impact on its surroundings? Not only does urban expansion bear strongly on environmental issues, but it is a matter for planning decision. It removes land from agricultural use and from large-scale open-air recreation. It also affects water systems in a big way. Urban areas create a demand for water, but at the same time may, in some circumstances, occupy the catchment area for its supply. They also create sewage that needs to be treated and then disposed of in a safe manner. The hard surfaces within urban areas increase what is known as "run off": large quantities of storm water that is not being absorbed by soil and vegetation and has to flow elsewhere, imposing the costs on those living downstream as a result of the measures needed for handling this flow safely and preventing flooding. River valleys may contain "flood plains" where storm water can be retained before flowing down stream. If they are built on, as they have been in the past, then these buildings may flood from time to time unless expensive defensive works are provided. These measures will then have the effect of forcing the water farther downstream, without it having a chance to be absorbed, imposing costs on more settlements. In addition to these serious issues with the quantity of water, there are those affecting it purity that are planning matters such as the location of industrial processes and other potentially polluting activities.

Urban areas also produce solid waste. Hopefully, reuse and recycling should serve to minimise the quantity of waste, but there will still be a lot to be disposed of. Location of incinerators for burning it is a controversial planning issue, even when they may also provide some electrical power as a by-product. Although now regarded as something to be avoided, waste continues to be sent to landfill and finding places to put it continues to be a planning challenge. Less well known, but still an issue, is what to do with sites that contain land-filled waste but are no longer in use for that purpose. The surface can be unstable and polluted. It may be grassed over, but the safe options for potential activities can be limited. All these are matters for planning that planners have to wrestle with.

PLANNING IN THE COUNTRYSIDE

In addition to the environmental impact of urban growth, there are plenty of other environmental issues within the countryside. The problem for planning within the countryside is that there are a number of competing users of the land and that their interests do not coincide but pull in opposite directions. There are at least four main uses to what people call "the countryside" can be put:

- farming;
- outdoor recreation;
- preserving particular landscapes, vegetation and animal life;
- providing places for people to live in pleasant surroundings.

Back in the early and mid-20th century, it was often thought that the first three would all pull together in the common interest but, sadly, this did not turn out to be the case.

The countryside as we see it now is rarely "natural" in that it has not been fashioned by human hand. There may be some areas where human activity has been comparatively minimal that need to be preserved for their scientific interest and, therefore, protected from urban development. This is a matter for planning decision. The countryside has been largely, but not exclusively shaped by agriculture. However, farmers are there to run a business for their own profit and to provide food for others to eat. They tend to be unsentimental about the aesthetic characteristics of rural areas and do not have a direct interest in setting land aside for scientific or cultural purposes. Agriculture now employs comparatively few people. There is a trend for more and more people to be employed in tourism in the countryside, as mentioned in the previous chapter, but the tourists come for rural scenery that may be more historic in nature rather than the product of contemporary farming. They may walk over crops, leave gates open or disturb farm animals. They may also disturb habitats preserved for scientific interest. In effect, the interests of agriculture, science and tourism are largely incompatible and may require separate allocations of land. On top of all this, there is the desire of better-off people to own their own house in the countryside, either as a second home for the holidays or as a permanent home linked to work by a long car journey or by driving to the to the station to take the train. They may complain about agricultural activities causing noise and smells, delays to traffic from agricultural vehicles on the roads and changing the picture-book scenery by the removal of trees and hedges. They will not be pleased either by being surrounded by large numbers of tourists either as holidaymakers or day-trippers, particularly as they will usually bring their cars with them. There are also people living in small villages and hamlets who are on low incomes. They face competition for houses from incomers, declining provision of shops and other services and sparser and more expensive bus services. Small businesses may want to relocate to rural areas, say in redundant farm buildings, but will they employ local people or will employees commute out from nearby towns?

Nevertheless, there is an enduring sentiment amongst the public at large that what they see as the countryside should be conserved for cultural and aesthetic reasons. There is, indeed, a lot to be said for this, just as there is for conservation in urban areas, but it also raises what can sometimes be seen as insuperable problems. Taking the question of conservation, just by itself, to start with. The problem is that the countryside has been in a constant state of change throughout history. What we see today is not what it was like centuries ago, and it may change substantially in the future. At what point do we stop the clock – as it is now, as it was fairly recently or at some time much further in the past? Alternatively, is it safe to allow it to evolve and, if so, how much change should be allowed? This is just the preliminary question.

It is the planner's task to allocate land uses so as somehow to reconcile these opposing interests. To some extent, this is possible to do this in places a long way from centres of population where there is sufficient space to give something to all interests. National parks may give priority to recreation and tourism. Scientific sites can be carefully protected from all comers. Areas of little aesthetic value can be devoted to modern agri-business. It is when and where all the interests described compete for the same pieces of land that the real challenges arise and where an optimum solution may not exist. This is a real, and on-going, challenge for the planning profession.

There has been a long tradition in planning policy of restraining building in the countryside, especially for new isolated houses, in pursuit of a clear distinction between town and country. Such policies can be strengthened by designating National Parks and areas of outstanding natural beauty. The original idea of national parks came from the USA, where they were primarily agricultural areas and were fairly remote from cities. However, in Britain they often contained agriculture, quarrying, small towns and villages and could be fairly close to major cities. Their designation was intended to give access for hikers for their health and recreation, but their numbers were soon overtaken by car-borne tourists. These tourists boosted the local economy but put adverse pressure on the environment they can come to experience. Planners can, and do, also designate areas of scientific interest, which can be protected from the effects of agriculture and tourism. Ideally, the planning system should also be able to get to grips with the issues surrounding rural housing and transport for the less well-off but, at the time of writing, this is rarely the case. This does not mean that the issues will go away, or that someone else is solving them, but that planners have to do their best to reconcile the conflicting interests within the limited means at their disposal.

COASTAL ISSUES

Particular planning issues arise for development along coasts. Some coastlines are subject to erosion, and the problem here is fairly clear cut. However, climate change is forecast to cause increases in sea levels that will initially be experienced as flooding during and after coastal storms. As with inland flooding, this raises the issue of whether development should be prohibited in potentially vulnerable areas or whether, alternatively, expensive sea defences should be constructed to protect it and, if they were, how long they would be effective for.

MINERAL EXTRACTION

One topic that is explicitly a planning matter in Britain is allocation of land for the extraction of minerals. Although opencast mining for coal and other minerals has been an issue for some particular localities, in 20th century and 21st century Britain, more commonly it is largely a matter of extracting stone, sand and gravel for use as building materials, for which increasing development means increasing demand. For the sand and gravel, this usually means digging in low-lying land within river valleys. All extraction competes for land with agriculture, recreation and urban development. It can also be seen as a bad neighbour to existing residential areas.

What will happen to the land after the minerals have been extracted? This may affect the decision on a new permission. Restitution would normally be required, but there is still the matter of the best use after this has been carried out. In dry agricultural areas, it would normally mean a return to farming at the extractor's expense. For gravel pits in river valleys, water-based recreation is a common solution.

There is also the question of what to do with historic mineral workings that are no longer in use. In dryer areas, old mineral workings have been used for landfill of waste. This can present two further problems. The trend is now against landfill on environmental grounds, and there is also the problem of what to do with the site once it is full, as referred to earlier in this chapter. Where there is much pressure for new building and land values therefore high, there is an incentive to use proceeds from development to help pay towards restitution and to integrate, where possible and advantageous, new buildings into the old workings. On the other hand, if land values are low then finding a solution may present a real challenge.

MORE BIG ISSUES – GETTING AROUND

DEALING WITH TRANSPORT IN URBAN AREAS

Transport matters are, and always have been, both a substantial and a very technical affair, so much so that that transport planning is often administered separately and can even be considered a separate professional activity. It is fundamental because of a two-way interaction. While the movement of people and goods is affected by how land uses are laid out, the transport facilities available will also affect how they are located. It is important because the location of human activities and the ease of getting around affect directly the quality of people's lives. Earlier in the book, we noted how the problems of the 19th century industrial city encouraged the growth of planning as it is currently understood. Such cities owed much of their structure to the development of mass public transport: horse buses, trams and suburban steam railways that enabled a large section of their population to live at some distance from their centres. Their economies depended on canals and railways for the movement of manufactured goods and raw materials. Although buses, trams and trains (but without their steam and horses) are still important in the contemporary city, its biggest challenges have arisen from the use of private motor vehicles.

THE MOTOR VEHICLE – FOR AND AGAINST

The use of motor vehicles to enable both goods and people to get around first became significant during the 1920s and 1930s, and by the middle of the 20th century, their impact was total. Their convenience made them very popular. They were available as and when you wanted to use them, and you could take them anywhere where roads were provided at public expense, which, in practice, meant almost anywhere. However, there were other consequences. Possession of a motor vehicle causes people to make more trips than they would do without it, for both people and goods. Their speed enables people and goods to travel farther afield within a given period of time. This has enabled land uses to become more spread out. Roads, junctions and car parks can take up large areas of land. Residential areas can be a long way from shops and places of work. Components used in manufacturing can be transported long distances between factories and so can the finished products destined for shops and customers. This uses more energy, and the use of energy per person or per tonne is not as efficient as, say, by rail. There is the problem of air pollution caused by the exhaust of internal combustion engines. However, whereas all these factors can increase costs, it appears that the convenience of motor vehicles is something people are prepared to pay for.

Looking at the private car in particular, there can be no doubt about its popularity, because of the huge increase in personal mobility its possession creates. It also provides personal entertainment and space for luggage. The fixed costs of owning one may be high: tax, insurance, maintenance, depreciation and so on, but once they are paid for, the marginal cost of each trip appears small, encouraging use. What then are the downsides? We have already noted air pollution, extravagant use of energy and the spreading out of land uses. Electric cars may ameliorate the first two problems, but the third is a fundamental issue for planning. If you look at the outer suburbs of cities in North America and Australasia, you see an urban form that is designed entirely around the use of the car for going to the shops, school, entertainment and work, as illustrated by Figure 5.1.

The way that these suburban areas are laid out makes them very difficult to serve by public transport. If a car is the only practical

Figure 5.1: Car-based "sprawl" in Helensvale, Queensland, Australia. Low-density housing is to the left and a shopping mall to the right. Note the amount of land taken up by motorways and surface car parking. (Ref: 13441-05 © Skyepics.com.au)

way of getting about, then this disadvantages those without access to one, particularly children and older people. Even in this modern age, not everyone has a driving licence. There is also a health problem. If a car is used for all journeys, then people may end up taking little exercise, leading to obesity and to other physical and mental health issues.

As important as these issues are, the one that has impacted most on planning as an activity is what to do about "congestion". Each motorist joining a road takes up space from others, and this slows the speed of the traffic. From the economist's point of view, each is imposing a cost on the others and, if they were all charged for it, then market forces would tend to regulate the numbers in proportion to the road space. However, from the motorist's point of view, road (and often parking) space being provided free at the point of use has long been taken for granted and drivers do not want this to change. What they want is more space provided at public expense to meet the ever-increasing demand. The motorist's view has, until comparatively recent times, resulted in the political line that congestion was a cost to the economy that could be removed by the supposed lesser cost of providing more and wider roads. The advantages of new roads were expressed in terms of time saved. When road vehicles go faster they take up more room because they drive farther apart. From the engineer's point of view, wider roads are needed to provide for these higher speeds rather than capacity for more vehicles. (Maximum throughput per lane occurs at slightly under 30 mph, 50 kph, so slower speeds can mean higher capacity.)

Unfortunately, no complete solution has ever been reached in practice. Most large cities in North America were rebuilt and extended with wide motorways and extensive car parks in pursuit of what was termed "full motorisation". However, in peak periods at least, their roads were, and still are, highly congested. Each new road, or new widening, filled up with traffic. Demand appeared insatiable. The fundamental problem is the amount of space that a car takes up compared to the size of a person. Ultimately, it becomes impossible to fit in all the cars. The roads and parking space necessary for all to be able to drive when and where they wish result in no space being left for the activities they are trying to get to, quite apart from the unacceptable cost to the taxpayer of the land and engineering works required. It is true that the "fight against congestion" is still pursued around the world as a political goal, but the problem is that it offers no prospect of winning.

A CHANGE IN ATTITUDE

A different attitude and gradual shift in public policy arose in Northwest Europe around the late 1960s and early 1970s. It eventually came to be accepted the demand for traffic flow and parking in town and city centres could not be met and, although it could not be eliminated, it could be restrained. Plans for urban motorway schemes were abandoned, not least because of public opposition to the cost and disruption they would cause. Pedestrian shopping streets were found to be both environmentally and commercially successful. Efforts were made to provide public transport of sufficient quantity and quality to enable those who wanted to reach urban centres without use of a car. Such efforts did not happen everywhere, nor all at once, and were not always completely successful. The point was that the direction of public policy had changed and was not reversed.

From the 1980s onwards, starting in Germany and the Netherlands, ideas began to develop further. The basic goal that speeds should be increased and journey times shortened was gradually being abandoned and was to be eventually stood on its head. What was now being advocated was that the goal of public policy should be enhanced environmental quality and that the easiest way to achieve this was to reduce, rather than increase, vehicle speeds. Slow vehicles are safer and less polluting. They take up less room, allowing road space to be reallocated to more environmentally beneficial uses as shown in Figure 5.2.

This can be enforced by the design of the road. So was born what became known, translating from the German, as "traffic calming". What was significant politically was that it did not involve "banning

Figure 5.2: Traffic calming in Groningen, the Netherlands, from the early 1990s. The carriageway for motor vehicles has been narrowed to one lane in each direction, reducing speed without resort to humps and ramps and creating space for a cycleway. A reservation allowing space for some short-term parking and bus stops separates the carriageway from the cyclists and pedestrians. (Tony Hall)

the car" but just making sure that it had to give way to the better quality of life in urban areas. The details and design implications of this approach will be set out in the next chapter.

Part and parcel of this new approach in European cities, and elsewhere, was the continued improvement in public transport. One notable example of this was the return of trams to many cities. Although there were some honourable exceptions, cities throughout the world abandoned their tram networks during the 1950s on the grounds that they were inflexible and contributed to traffic congestion. However, in the latter part of the 20th century, trams were brought back in many cities, although often with a far better vehicle design than those of the past, as shown by the example in Figure 5.3.

Most large cities throughout the world depend on electric underground and suburban railways to function. Electrified tracked systems are generally cheaper to run, less polluting and more popular with passengers than motor buses. However, they are very expensive to construct and need a lot of users in order to justify this cost.

Figure 5.3: A large modern tram in Mulhouse, France. (Tony Hall)

DEALING WITH GOODS VEHICLES

For the transport of goods, it is difficult to avoid the use of motor vehicles. Although it is desirable to make use of rail and water transport where possible, particularly for heavy and bulky goods, road vehicles are still needed at each end of the journey. Heavy goods vehicles present their own special problems because of their size and, most importantly, their weight. Generally, we are talking about axle weights, as this is where the weight impacts upon the road surface, although when a vehicle goes over a bridge it is the whole weight that has to be supported by the structure. As axle weight increases, its impact on the road surface does not go up in simple proportion but increases by many times. One heavy goods vehicle may, therefore, have an impact on the road equivalent to a very large number of cars, each of which is very light in comparison. A road that is only going to be used by cars can be light in construction and fairly cheap to build and maintain. On the other hand, roads that cater for heavy goods vehicles have to be very strong and will be expensive to both build and maintain. They also have to be wide with large turning circles. On the other hand, the character of streets depends on their intimacy and enclosure of space by buildings and trees. This creates a challenge for the design of urban areas because to have all roads capable of bearing heavy goods vehicles would destroy this character. Planners may have to work out special routes for heavy goods vehicles, apply restrictive times for delivery and make attempts where possible for bulk freight to be moved on rail or water. These solutions can be very important when dealing with aggregates for large construction projects and the disposal of bulk waste. Freight transport is not just a matter of items moving from factory to warehouse to shops, but of raw material moving to factories.

CAN THERE BE AN OVERALL PLANNED SOLUTION?

For planning, the key challenge is that it is not physically possible for all journeys at all times to be made by car, although doubtless some always will be. A question frequently put by car owners is how then do people get around, both now and in the future? In reality, a lot of people have to get around without a car anyway. We must note for a start that not all persons have a driving licence. Children are not allowed them and throughout the population possession is skewed away from women and older people. Furthermore, a very substantial minority of households, around a third, do not own a car. Surveys from the 1970s to the present day have found that, when presented with a high level of public transport provision and possible restrictions on car use that, whereas older people already driving are reluctant to give up use of their car, young people tend to postpone purchase and use of their first vehicle, most likely influenced by the high fixed costs involved. We can also note that owners of cars may not use them all the time. For example, most people travelling to work in central London do so by public transport even though they may have a car at home. Many trips are made entirely by walking or cycling, and car trips may involve walking at one end of the journey.

The question that has to be asked in planning practice is does the infrastructure and layout of urban and rural areas allow people to get where they want to go, with both convenience and minimum use of energy, without a car? As a first priority, can people get about using so-called "active" transport – walking and cycling? The reason why it should be the first priority is that it is good for personal health, cheap and minimises use of energy. Clearly the scale of cities precludes walking and cycling everywhere by everyone and so the second priority should be local public transport, i.e. buses, trams and suburban trains. In particular, it should enable people to get to long-distance transport facilities such as express trains and airports. Note that, so far, we have not mentioned "getting people out of their cars", or "modal transfer" to give it a very technical name. We are talking about designing urban and rural areas so, ideally, people can get around even if they have no car. Over and above this, it may well be a very good idea to provide ways by which car drivers may find it easy to change to other modes of travel or combine driving with them. Most familiar of these are "park and ride" facilities, where car parks are provided on the edge of towns and cities with good quality bus links into the urban area.

Unfortunately, planners do not control directly the policies of public transport operators nor the bodies making provision for motorways and trunk roads and for airports. However, they can negotiate with them and pursue incremental improvements through control of design of new development. Trying to get bus stations and railway stations next to each other and next to shopping and commercial centres is not exactly a new idea, and it is something that can be strived for all the time. Planning policy can also resist the loss of these facilities to commercial development.

When negotiating and approving large, new residential schemes, planners can influence the design of roads to reduce traffic speeds and re-allocate road space to other uses, as referred to earlier in this chapter. The re-development of shopping and commercial areas of city centres also offers opportunity to reduce road space in favour of other uses, and this can, perhaps surprisingly, be supported by major commercial interests. There have been a growing number of examples of the removal of sections of 1960s ring, and inner relief, roads together with flyovers, and replacing them with standard roads with conventional traffic lights and pedestrian crossings. Over time, they had begun to be seen as creating a barrier for access to, and expansion of, the central commercial and retail area and to sterilise potentially valuable land. One of the most important British examples has been the removal of the elevated western section of the Birmingham inner ring road in 2002, which permitted the subsequent reallocation of road space to substantial new commercial development.

How then to get some overall solution? A lack of expertise is not the problem. A lot of people spend a lot of time in solving transport problems ranging from design of roads and vehicles to levels of fares and subsidies. Much technical knowledge is required to make forecasts and find technical solutions. All this is very important, but what we are thinking about here is how transport issues fit into planning ones. Effective planning requires thinking positively over a wider planning canvas rather than just talking about technical transport solutions. As with other planning issues, it is fundamentally a matter of values because it has a direct effect on the well-being of different groups in society – the young, the old, men, women and people with different income levels. The search is for optimum solutions and, fortunately, they appear to be within reach.

6

THE MEDIUM STUFF – WHERE TO PUT THINGS?

THE DESIGN AND LAYING OUT OF URBAN AREAS

We have seen in the previous chapters that planning has not been able to adequately solve all the really big problems at the grand scale – how to deal with land values such that there will be sufficient and affordable houses within reach of sufficient jobs, all properly served by transport facilities and other services. On the other hand, we have also noted that planning systems are popular throughout the world, even in cases where their effectiveness appears to be very limited. Why should this be so? The reason is that there still has to be a planning system in place to make decisions on where development is to be located and how much of it in any given place. "Non-plan" is not an option. There are some very important reasons why planning as a professional activity is still needed in the absence of progress on long-term strategic goals. Decisions need to be made on the location of housing estates, office blocks, hospitals, schools, parks, warehouses, factories, roads, railways and so on. There is an analogy with medicine here. Patients still need to be cared for, even when the nature of, and treatment for, a disease may not be fully known.

The first reason why people say they want a planning system is that activities on land affect their daily lives. They affect both the people actually engaged in these activities and also people living and working around them. For example, a school has pupils, teachers and also support staff. People living around it may view it in two ways. They may see it as desirable because it educates their children. On the other hand, they may see the children, and car traffic generated by it at certain times of the day, as nuisances and, therefore, they do not want to be near a school. However, even if they see the school as a nuisance, they may also get benefit from it if their house looks out on to its playing fields rather than other houses. The location of a new school can, therefore, easily give rise to controversy because it impacts upon a complex web of interests. Although "planning" might attempt to arrive at the "best" location for a school on technical grounds – such as maximum walking distance for the children – there is always going to be a debate between the interested parties involved, and this process has to be managed in some way. The same will also apply to many other land uses, not just schools.

The second reason is that any new development does not take place on a blank sheet. There are usually existing buildings, roads, parks and so on. People might see some as very special and needing to be kept, such as picturesque landscapes in the countryside and historic areas of towns. Even if they do not, the impact of new development upon existing buildings and landscape has to be considered as a long-term issue. They will still be there long after the existing users, and their neighbours have moved on. For an existing urban area, the impact of new development can be a complex one. It can be visual, or one of noise and pollution, but it does not necessarily have to be negative. A new building can be beautiful and enhancing. It is not just the impact on the immediate surroundings that matters. Some consequences, such as traffic generated, may be felt over a wide area. All this has to be managed. The development process cannot just be left to its own devices, or so the consensus around the world on the need for planning systems seems to say.

What all this saying is that there are important practical goals at this scale – both in terms of the general level of amenity and how a place looks and feels. Buildings and the spaces they create last a long time and so these goals will embody issues of heritage – what should be kept for later generations.

RESTORING PROSPERITY

Planning can play a very important role in restoring prosperity (and also restoring the buildings, streets and parks, which is not quite the same thing) to places that have seen better days, a process known as "regeneration". It is a process where there can, in some circumstances, be substantial and visible progress within ten years or so. However, there may also be some downsides, as we shall see. It is a process that requires vision – an idea of what a place down on its luck could really become – something that local people can find very difficult. It also requires negotiation – a lot of different organisations have to be brought on side – not just to support the vision but also to put their own money into realising it.

Areas of cities may go into decline because of structural changes in the national and international economy. In Chapter 3, we talked about such changes, particularly the example of the decline of manufacturing industry. A large firm that has been in an area for a long time may employ local people who, in turn, spend money in local shops and on local services. If the main local employer shuts down, then this has a knock-on effect on other local businesses. The trade of local shops can also be affected by changes in retailing – a large new supermarket elsewhere in the city can take away trade and force local shops to close. Less jobs locally means that people move away and that those that remain may have less money to spend on their houses. The local council gets less income in rates and taxes from the area. Vacant properties become derelict. Unemployed youth may turn to crime. A vicious circle of decline may develop. Sometimes, such an area may contain buildings, parks and squares of historic value, but there is no longer the money to maintain them. They are used less and less and fall into disrepair. On the other hand, poorer parts of cities can have advantages for some. Land values are low, and this is to the advantage of people looking to set up a small new private business, such as a restaurant or café or a small shop. It can also be of use to those working in the creative and performing arts, including popular music, who need a lot of space, say for recording and rehearsals or for painting, but do not have a lot of money.

To restore prosperity, the idea is to get people to spend money in a locality, either as visitors or as residents. This should, hopefully, benefit local businesses who will then employ more people and who, in turn, will spend money locally creating a virtuous circle. The process can be greatly helped if the area has buildings of architectural value or landscape features, such as waterfronts, with the potential to be made attractive to people. If such features are restored, they could attract tourists and/or new residents with money to spend. These buildings and landscape features could be restored with public money, as a pump-priming initiative, and/or money from private developers. Once people start to come, then developers and businesses will likely be attracted because there is money to be made. Planning has a role in facilitating this process and providing the initial vision. Where there are no existing features of architectural or landscape value, there is still a role for investment to create new ones – it is just more challenging.

The process by which new and better-off residents move in and start doing up the houses is known as "gentrification". It can lead to the restoration of historic buildings with private money and for creating a demand for new shops and services, but it also has a downside. A gentrified locality will look attractive and prosperous, but there are some important questions to be asked when assessing its success. What has happened to the poorer people who used to live there? What has happened to the creative activities and their artistic, recording and rehearsal space? In many cases, there are brand new shopping complexes, but they are now filled with standard chain stores. What has happened to the independent retailers and restaurants? The answer is that in all these cases land values have risen and they cannot afford the new rents. This takes us back to the land value issues we discussed when tackling the "big stuff". Gentrification need not be a problem if there is also a housing policy to cater for those on lower incomes city-wide and if cheaper, perhaps subsidised, locations are provided elsewhere for business start-ups. Again, we see that to be successful, planning is, inevitably, complex. It involves negotiations with many parties and, in the end, is determined by the political process. It is not just a matter of roads and buildings.

PLANNING FOR SHOPPING

Dealing with shops is one of planning's biggest challenges. A particular problem is that, in the medium to long term, the whole nature of shopping can change. For example, the second half of the 20th century saw the growth of larger and larger shops surrounded by extensive car parks. These then coalesced into large indoor shopping centres surrounded by even more extensive car parks, as in the example to be seen in Figure 5.1. This represented a change in the economics of shopping and reflected, and encouraged, a move to a car-based suburban lifestyle. The only places where there was usually room for such shopping centres were on the edges of, or outside of, existing urban areas. Such centres were not easily accessible by those without access to a car, particularly the very young and very old. Although some larger town centres could hold their own in competition with such new shopping facilities, smaller ones and suburban centres could not compete and experienced a fall in trade. Loss of traditional shopping provision in this way not only disadvantaged some particular, less mobile, sections of society, but represented a loss of quality of urban life that many people valued.

From the 2010s onwards, internet shopping started to make a difference, not just by enabling buying online but also by making home delivery more efficient and, therefore, cheaper. This can lead, in the right places, to older centres re-establishing themselves as places for shopping as a leisure pursuit. Traditional streets that have been pedestrianised, have had attractive buildings done up, and now feature shops combined with restaurants and entertainment facilities can provide this.

There is an additional problem that arises when groups of small shops are provided in a new development. In older areas there will be businesses that have been there for a long time and, especially if the area is not too prosperous, and commercial rents may be low. On the other hand, on new estates the higher cost of land and investment in new buildings makes it difficult for small businesses to afford the rents. This can result in there being only chain shops and thus a restricted range of choice. Restrictions on development in existing urban areas can keep rents low and make it easier for small family-owned businesses, but they may be seen in some circles as holding back growth, prosperity and modernisation. Regeneration and improvement of an area may bring in more trade, but complete rebuilding can push up rents and make it difficult for independent small shops to survive.

Most people would say that they would want a mixture of different types of shop on a scale that fits well into the neighbourhood. There is much to be said for this in planning terms, but the challenge is how it is to be brought about when the commercial forces driving change are outside of the planners' control. The problem for planners is the economic forces changing the nature of shopping. Planners can normally exercise only negative controls such as preventing the building of new large stores or the conversion of existing shops, i.e. stopping things happening. They have few powers to make shops come into an area. However, planning is not just a matter of legal powers. Planners can negotiate with large retailers. They can encourage them to move in to localities where redevelopment is contemplated. They can use their judgement when thinking about the effect of new development, which they do control, on rents for shops. This is an area where planners have to be aware of social and economic trends and take account of them when negotiating new schemes. They have to try to play a weak hand to best advantage for neighbourhoods, villages, towns and cities as a whole.

HANDLING LOCAL TRAFFIC

The problem of the private motor vehicle is that it is land hungry. The space for roads, car parks and garages uses up a considerable amount of land. The extent of this land pushes the activities upon it farther apart and creates barriers between them. This severance increases with vehicle speed. High vehicle speeds can only be maintained safely if roads are wide and pedestrians are kept at a distance. This results in public areas that are unpleasant to look at and suffer from noise and air pollution. How then can urban areas be designed to allow for access by cars without these disadvantages?

One way is to reduce the impact of motor vehicles through the use of circuitous routing and cul-de-sacs to remove through trips, particularly residential areas, as shown in Figure 6.1.

However, this increases severance, and therefore walking times, and makes it very difficult to make deliveries to dwellings and to serve them by buses. It also makes it difficult for people to find their way.

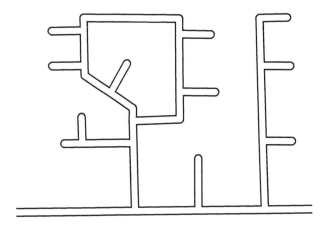

Figure 6.1: A residential street layout dominated by extended cul-de-sacs. While offering seclusion to residents, it is problematic for buses and service vehicles and makes it difficult to find your way. (Tony Hall)

A more advantageous approach is to restrict the speed of the vehicle. As explained in the previous chapter, slow vehicles are safer and less polluting. They take up less room, allowing road space to be reallocated to more environmentally beneficial uses. Speed limits imposed by laws and signs alone can be difficult to enforce, but roads can be designed such that it is near to impossible for motor vehicles to exceed a specific speed. The situation becomes self-enforcing. This approach was developed in Germany and the Netherlands during the 1980s and became known, from the literal translation of its German name, as *traffic calming.* It then spread from these countries to other parts of Northwest Europe during the 1990s and thence to the rest of Europe and other parts of the world.

The first design solutions were developed for very low speeds, almost walking pace, as illustrated by Figure 6.2.

The use of, say, speed humps alone to achieve slow speeds did not realise the true potential of traffic calming. What was important was the release of road space for other uses. This space could be for the benefit of the motorist through provision of additional parking but, more commonly, it was used for the benefit of cyclists

Figure 6.2: A very low-speed traffic-calming scheme, or "Woonerf" in Dutch, in Delft, the Netherlands, from the early 1980s. Note how planting and paving is used to good effect and how parking is fitted in. (Tim Pharoah)

and pedestrians. The distinguishing feature was an overall environmental enhancement through the employment of quality paving and planting, although this could work out very expensive. In residential areas, it often became more cost-effective to introduce 20 mph (30 kph) zones where large areas could be covered more cheaply, but with the comparatively higher traffic speed, as in the early example illustrated in Figure 6.3.

Traffic calming solutions could also be applied to shopping streets, as illustrated in Figure 6.4.

The beginning of the 21st century in Northwest Europe saw these ideas being taken much further with the introduction of *shared surfaces* used by all road users (motor vehicles, cyclists and pedestrians) without restriction, coupled with the removal of all signs and traffic signals. The idea was that motorists adjust their behaviour and drive slowly and cautiously when amongst pedestrians. The approach can be used to particular advantage in predominantly pedestrianised shopping streets, where a limited number of service vehicles and

Figure 6.3: A 30 kph (20 mph) zone in Heerde, the Netherlands, from the early 1980s. (Tim Pharoah)

Figure 6.4: A traffic-calmed shopping area, or "Winkelerf" in Dutch, in Rijswijk, Den Haag, the Netherlands, from the early 1980s. (Tim Pharoah)

Figure 6.5: A well-regarded "shared surface" scheme in Brighton, Sussex, from 2007. (Tim Pharoah)

taxis can be allowed. Re-paving can bring about a great improvement in appearance and better use of available space. This approach is not without controversy, particularly from those representing the blind and partially sighted. Nevertheless, schemes have been implemented in shopping streets and at urban traffic intersections in many locations in Northwest Europe. The original schemes in the Netherlands, and other parts of Europe, have reported a reduction in accident rates. A British example for a historic tourist area is illustrated in Figure 6.5.

CREATING LOCAL PLACES

Bringing all matters of building and street design together at the local scale takes us to a particular aspect of planning often known as "urban design". Just like "town planning", "urban design" is a catch-all word that covers a variety of important activities. At the time of writing, "placemaking" was increasingly being used as a more precise term to convey what "urban design" is really getting at. It deals with the outdoor spaces created by buildings and trees – what they look like and how they are used. Many professional activities: architecture, landscape architecture, civil engineering, surveying and so on may be involved, not just planning. It is often misunderstood by the public as being just a matter of the appearance of buildings and landscapes – a judgement about whether they are beautiful or not – and that all this is just a matter of opinion with different individuals and groups being entitled to their own ideas. However, this is far from the case. To start with, having pleasant, if not beautiful surroundings is a basic human need that can be addressed in a systematic way. What is more important, though, is that urban design addresses a number of other human needs that are very practical and clear cut. Most important is being safe and secure, followed closely by the ability to be sociable, meeting other people for both business and pleasure. There is also the very practical matter of being able to find your way. Urban design can deal with all these issues in a positive manner.

Interestingly, having pleasant surroundings and being able to find your way can be comparatively less controversial than ways of achieving security and sociability. It has been found that people find urban spaces attractive where they are visually enclosed by buildings or trees. This can be done in lots of different ways and, in fact, having a variety of different spaces is very important for both pleasurable surroundings and wayfinding. If one examines cities around the world that are renowned for their beauty, and their success as tourist centres, then this is what you see. Coupled with the use of landmarks, this also helps with wayfinding – people remember the urban spaces they pass through on different journeys. It can be rationalised and formulated into a systematic method, often called "townscape" analysis, that produces results that can be helpful in the design of urban areas.

Although sociability and security may, at first sight, appear hard and fast concepts that everybody would consider desirable, as opposed to whether things look beautiful, in reality, they are the ones that can be more contentious when it comes to laying out new urban development. It is here that a "planned environment" implies definite physical solutions that are based on a definite choice of values. The argument is that streets, squares, parks, suburban roads, shops and so on should be so designed, and so linked together, that there is the maximum chance of people being around all the time. This is clearly going to maximise sociability, but the argument is that it will also maximise security. People will look out for each other and will be deterred from crime if others are watching. Furthermore, people in the street should be visible from within the buildings and should be able to see at least some activity within the same buildings. The more that people are seen and can see others, the more secure they will feel. This is not to say that all spaces and streets must be busy and bustling. There should be a variety of urban spaces, some busy and some quiet. However, even if you are talking about a quiet walk in the park then you will still want to see at least a few other people around to feel safe.

Whereas this is the view associated with the practice of planning and urban design, there is another popular view which is in direct conflict with it. People say "wouldn't it be nice if I could live right down the end of a long cul-de-sac. I would see almost no traffic and it would be very quiet. As there would be very few people around there would be very few criminals and other undesirables hanging about". The attraction of the idea is plain to see. Everyone needs peace and quiet at some time. The problem is that it is not as safe as it sounds. It is much easier for burglars to operate if there is hardly anyone around. If you are attacked who will be there to help you? In addition, if everybody over a whole city lives their lives not encountering others and seeing people only by appointment, it is hardly going to be a happy fun place. In addition, as we have already noted, patterns of streets that consist predominantly of long cul-de-sacs are difficult to serve by buses, and for deliveries and make it very difficult for people to find their way. These are the reasons why type of layout shown in Figure 6.1 would not now be considered satisfactory in planning terms.

This is not to say that there should be no space for quiet enjoyment and privacy, far from it. Urban design principles can provide a physical solution here in terms of "public fronts" and "private backs" for buildings. In the public street, as we have said, people can meet each other and feel safe as a result. At the back, there is quiet and privacy and safety here comes from protection from the surrounding buildings, as shown in Figure 6.6.

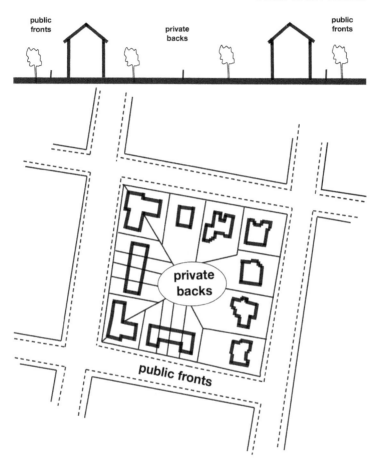

Figure 6.6: Perimeter blocks creating public fronts and private backs to buildings. (Tony Hall)

What we have here is an optimum solution balancing peoples' need for sociability with need for privacy. It leads to an interrelated grid of streets rather than the layout shown in Figure 6.1. (The word "grid" here does not necessarily imply the use of straight roads and right-angled corners, or that there will always be a through route for motor vehicles, but refers to the pattern of movement open to pedestrians.) This is a practical result. It is not new. It has always worked in the past and is reflected in our traditional layout of buildings and streets.

Urban design, or placemaking, is a topic where professional planning has something to say – an explicit message putting forward definite values. It can be expressed as a choice between two packages. In the first, there is little actual planning intervention. The arrangement of buildings, roads and public spaces is determined by convenience of access by car as the first consideration. Security comes from being indoors or in a car. Unfortunately, it is not very nice to look at or pleasant to walk around in outside nor is it easy to meet people casually. In the second package, cars can still be used, but access takes second place to quality of the public areas. Top priority is given to the area being nice to look at and to making it pleasant to walk around outside and easy to meet people. Buildings and planting are arranged to create this. Security comes from having other people around.

7

THE SMALL STUFF – THE DAY-TO-DAY BUT IMPORTANT WORK OF THE PLANNING OFFICE

A large proportion of the work of a typical planning office is rarely written about in textbooks or discussed in general books about planning's role in society. This work is largely the "small stuff", minor matters affecting individual households, shops or other small businesses, or issues affecting local streets and other spaces. For all of its small scale, this work is none the less important, and it is an area where planning can arguably claim more success than at the broader scale. The issues that the planning system has to make decisions on at this scale include

- extensions of premises;
- change of detailed appearance of premises;
- change of use of premises;
- provision, replacement and protection, as appropriate, of watercourses and trees and other vegetation.

The reasons why these decisions should be seen as important and a matter of "planning" are as follows:

- they can have a cumulative effect on the appearance and function of public areas;

- an individual building or tree may be around for a very long time;
- particular items of long-term value may need to retained and protected for future generations;
- even a small alteration can affect the amenity of a neighbouring property.

These local decisions also provide the opportunity to achieve positive long-term outcomes by improvements on a bit-by-bit basis. A point that needs to be stressed is that, whereas opportunities to design new large-scale schemes occur only occasionally, small changes are happening all the time, and, if there is a long-term policy to guide them, enable overall improvements to be made to a locality in the longer term.

TYPES OF SMALL PLANNING ISSUES

What types of planning issue give rise to the work covered by this "small stuff"? We can consider a number of examples.

HOUSE EXTENSIONS

First, let us think about extensions to houses, most often to the rear but also to the side and, occasionally, to the front. There are a number of questions for the planning officer to consider. Will the additional structure have an overbearing effect on the neighbouring properties, even causing a loss of natural light? Will the position of the windows result in overlooking and loss of privacy for the neighbours? Will sufficient space, including the garden, be left around the house, particularly at the rear? If the extension is to the front, will it have an impact on the look of the street? Whether or not action can be taken on any of these points will depend on current legislation and on local planning policy, both of which are subject to change over time. Our purpose here is to draw attention to the general issues which are not necessarily the same as the legal powers at any given moment. For example, the size of the extension (in proportion to the existing house) that may require planning permission will be laid down in legislation and government regulations. The exact proportion may change over time, but the fact will remain that this relationship is an issue that has to be considered.

The example shown in Figure 7.1 is not put forward necessarily as an acceptable proposal, although it will appear to many as not too unreasonable, but to illustrate the issues with which the planner is faced.

Would the reader consider it to be acceptable in the light of the points made above? Should the windows looking out over the neighbour's garden have obscure glazing? Supposing the extension stretched further down the back garden – how far would be acceptable? How much garden should be retained? Could it go higher than the existing house or should it really be much lower? What about restriction of light to existing windows? Supposing all the houses were to want the same type of extension, what would be the overall effect? Whereas these are not matters of grand planning strategy,

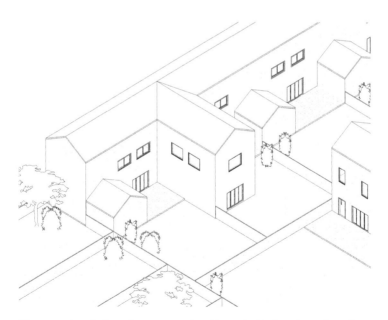

Figure 7.1: A typical rear house extension. (drawn by Nathan Ominski under the direction of the author.)

decisions made on individual cases can have a significant impact of the lives of ordinary people.

ADDITIONAL HOUSES

The next example is the construction of a new house or, perhaps, several houses to the side, or to the rear, of existing buildings, often known as "infill". The questions that need to be asked include all those we have listed above for house extensions, plus some additional ones. An additional dwelling, or dwellings, means that there will be an additional entrance, or entrances from the road, for both people and motor vehicles. Provision of new accesses may turn a fence between gardens into one that is open on one side, possibly reducing security and feelings of privacy. Other issues are how will a car get on to the public road and how will these arrangements affect the safety and appearance? These points are illustrated in Figure 7.2.

As with the previous figure, the two houses shown as "backland" development are not put forward as necessarily acceptable, although many readers may judge their impact to be small. The point is to draw attention to the issues that the planner has to, or ought to, think about.

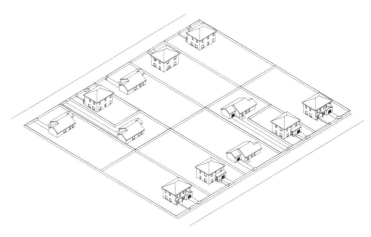

Figure 7.2: A low-density residential area with sporadic back-land development. (drawn by Nathan Ominski under the direction of the author.)

Whereas one or two houses might not have too great impact in themselves, if more infill is proposed over time, then local controversy and issues of planning policy will certainly arise. If a significant number of new houses are proposed, how will this sit with any policies about the density of houses and flats in the area? Even where there is no official development plan policy on this topic for this location, it is something that local people will be concerned about. Depending on local circumstances, where there is a policy, it may seek an increase in density as part of a wider planning strategy. In, for example, a low-density residential area with detached houses on large plots, an occasional house inserted to the rear of a plot may not be seen as raising many problems. On the other hand, if this were to be repeated over and over again, then the density would gradually increase over time changing the general character of the area and the way that it functions in terms of traffic circulation. But there is more to it than this. Here we come to a subtler issue. Even if the overall planning policy sought an increase in density, one or two badly placed houses could frustrate a properly planned high-density housing scheme for the area.

A range of possible scenarios is illustrated in Figures 7.3–7.5. Again, they show what planning policy, professional judgment and political decision-making have to contend with. Some of the proposals shown may be more or less acceptable depending on local policy. Some are, indeed, more reflective of the desirable design principles discussed in the previous chapter. However, quite a lot of what is shown would generally be seen as a "bad thing".

Figure 7.3 shows what can happen in the absence of strong local policy and the ability of developers to buy and amalgamate existing plots into a larger developable area. Two plots have been brought together but not others. Problems with appearance and security are now more numerous. A particular issue with the new houses is the exposed rear fences backing on to the main road. The issue overall is not just that the density is increasing as such but because it is happening in an unplanned and sporadic manner. Problems affecting individual houses and plots begin to proliferate.

In Figure 7.4, the developer has managed to acquire and amalgamate the land at the rear of many of the properties and acquire a strip of land to provide access for motor vehicles. This avoids

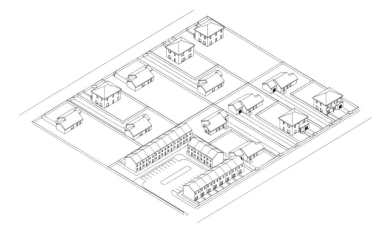

Figure 7.3: A low-density residential area with further back-land development and two plots amalgamated to accommodate a higher-density scheme with terrace houses. (drawn by Nathan Ominski under the direction of the author.)

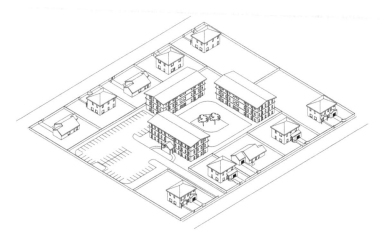

Figure 7.4: A low-density residential area with back-land gardens amalgamated to accommodate a high-density, and out-of-scale, scheme with flats. (drawn by Nathan Ominski under the direction of the author.)

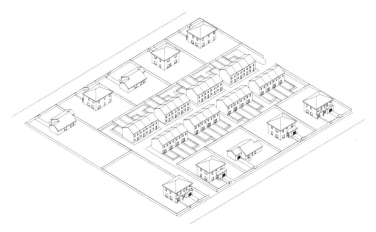

Figure 7.5: A low-density residential area with back-land gardens amalgamated to accommodate a higher-density scheme with terrace houses but with better regard for contemporary urban design principles. (drawn by Nathan Ominski under the direction of the author.)

sporadic and uncoordinated development over time. However, the blocks of flats shown would certainly prove controversial. Obviously, there is the question of the visual impact on surrounding properties to be considered. Even if this was judged acceptable, what ought to be in people's minds is "is this to be a one-off scheme or will the whole area be rebuilt in the same manner in the fullness of time?". Whether or not there is going to be pressure from developers for this is a matter of forecasting trends in the price of land. To control, it requires a planning policy. A procedural means to control density would be a fairly straightforward matter. (It was provided for in the 1947 Act development plans for towns, but not counties). The debate has turned on whether to do so would be desirable. From time to time, central governments have taken different views about whether local planning policy should, or should not, restrict it.

Figure 7.5 shows the same developable piece of land but with the "urban design" principles advanced in the previous chapter applied to the layout of the houses. There may still be security issues with the access roads (will they be secluded alleyways at night with few people around?) and so we are not saying here that the proposal is completely acceptable. What we are trying to illustrate the issues that planning has to grapple with.

CHANGE OF USE

Now let us think about the change of use of an existing building, as opposed to the construction of a new one, and, in particular, changes from house to shop or small business, shop to house, or between different types of small shop.

Let us take, as an example, the conversion of a house in a predominantly residential area. Generally, a lot of opposition can be expected from local residents. There will be concerns about an increase in the number of people, particularly those that may congregate outside, and, more importantly, increase in traffic and number of parked cars. There is also the matter of service vehicle access for deliveries and other purposes. Some uses such as a doctor or dental surgery may be considered more acceptable. A convenience store or small café might be accepted by local residents if they already exist, but not as a new proposal. Proposals for large restaurants and bars will raise issues of potential noise and odours from cooking. In addition to these matters, all the design requirements for new houses, as discussed above, will also apply.

At first sight, this might seem to suggest that it is converting houses to shops, which raises all the issues. However, there can be problems in the other direction. Conversion of a local pub or corner shop into a house may be seen by local people as the loss of something valuable and be resisted. There are also issues raised by converting premises from one type of shop to another. An antiques shop or clothes shop might have a fairly low intensity of use compared to a food and drink outlet, particularly of the take-away variety, and all the other issues presented by conversion from a house will also apply. However, a village full of antique shops but no food outlets will clearly be at a disadvantage. In a major town, although banks and estate agents are necessary, whole lines of them can change the whole character of an existing shopping street and, if they thereby drive out food shops, then this can be a real problem. Conversion to a betting or sex shop may raise public debate about desirability, but these types of premises are usually governed by other legislation, which is as it should be.

TREES

Moving on to an apparently quite different example, let us look at the subject of trees. Why should there be a planning issue? To start with, they are very important for the appearance of a locality. In particular, they enclose spaces, just as buildings do and are important for the appearance of streets, squares and other urban spaces. They also have an important environmental role:

- they contribute to a beneficial local microclimate, providing both shade and moisture;
- along with other vegetation, they help to control the absorption and flow of storm water;
- they are also important in maintaining biodiversity in urban areas, notably for bird life;
- they contribute feelings of health and well-being.

Looking carefully at the scene in Figure 7.6, we can see the important contribution that trees can make to the attractiveness of an area, and, less visibly, its biodiversity and microclimate. Trees live for a long time and may take many years to grow to maturity. Putting all these considerations together, it can be seen why they are an important part of a planner's job. Their planting and retention need to be properly managed.

What can planners actually do here? At the most basic level, they can prevent trees being cut down if they have sufficient justification to put a legal order on them. They cannot just be any tree but must have special merit. Ideally, they should contribute to the look of the place in an important way. A legal order is one thing but enforcing it is another, and this is much easier if the tree concerned is on public land. If a tree is in someone's back garden, then enforcement is going to be much more difficult. There may be penalties for cutting it down, but once it is gone, it is gone.

The other thing that planners can do is to encourage the provision of trees, and other vegetation, in new development, and they may

Figure 7.6: The role of trees and their protection. A large oak tree has been deliberately retained as a central feature in the late 1970s housing scheme at Galleywood Paddock, Chelmsford, Essex. (Tony Hall)

require a developer to present a landscaping scheme for approval. When negotiating permission for new buildings, especially a large housing scheme, they can try to make sure that they respect existing trees of particular value as well as planting new ones.

HERITAGE

The importance of all the factors discussed above can be heightened if the buildings, or the locality as a whole, are of architectural or historical importance. What some might see as relatively minor question, such as the colour they are to be painted, and alterations to windows and doors, can actually be important issues.

As a starting point, we can think just about individual buildings. Should they be protected from demolition? Should their internal layout be protected from changes? What about external painting and alterations to windows and doors? There are a number of questions that have to be addressed. Does the building have special historic importance? Was it associated with particular historic events or a famous person? Alternatively, or in addition, does it have any

special architectural importance? Was it designed by a famous ar-
chitect or was it a remarkable example of the style of a particular
period or a method of construction? All these points are matters
of judgement, and there will be often room for different opinions.
However, there will likely be widespread public concern for the
building's preservation and, in support of this, a whole range of experts and documents that can be consulted. If a case is made, then a
legal order can be obtained to protect the building from demolition
or alteration. It is important to stress that this does not mean that no
changes will be permitted. From time to time, some alterations are
usually justified and, in extreme cases, even demolition may, reluc-
tantly, be allowed. This is an area for judgement by planning and
architectural professionals and other experts, with the final decision
being a local political one. Why, then, might change be allowed?
One example is the restoration and making safe of a building that
has been neglected and has decayed. Another is removing additions
or changes to the building that had been made before it was protected. This can be tricky in practice because historic buildings have
often gathered additions and alterations ever since they were first
built. Returning a building to "square one" might involve loss of
many of its special features in addition to those that are not worthy
of its historic or architectural value.

The role of planning in heritage issues goes beyond individual
buildings. There is the wider issue of a building's "context". The reason why people value, and visit as tourists, historic areas is because of
the way that their buildings fit together to provide an overall effect.
Also, it is not just the buildings. Paving, trees, colour and texture
of materials can all be very important. To maintain the overall effect, it is often necessary to prevent the demolition of, and control
the external appearance of, particular buildings that, although not
meriting protection in their own right, make an important contribution to the total composition. This all comes under the heading of
"conservation". "Conservation" is distinct from "preservation". The
latter implies that there will be no change while the former means
that there will be change but that it will be managed while still
maintaining the overall effect.

This leads on to the issue of the replacement of buildings in such
areas that are of little value in themselves, make no contribution to

the overall effect, or may even be highly intrusive and detract from the overall attractiveness. In some cases, a new building in an exact and scholarly reproduction of an older style may be appropriate but not always so. In some other cases, one in a more modern style which, nevertheless, reflects its historic context may be appropriate. As with all planning issues, this becomes a matter for professional judgement and political decision.

We have used the words "historic" and "heritage" here, but it would be wrong to give the impression that we are always talking about very old streets and buildings. Areas that have been built comparatively recently also deserve consideration. Buildings can last a long time, and the task can be one of achieving continuity with the best aspects of what has gone before. Context is very important when deciding on whether to allow infill by new houses, offices or shops in any area. Designs that do not respect the proportions, doors, windows, materials and other aspects of appearance of existing buildings can cause problems. Again, this does not necessarily mean that they must reproduce exactly the inner structure or outward style of the older buildings. In many cases, a contemporary building that respects the proportions and position in the street of the existing buildings may fit it, as illustrated in the example shown in Figure 7.7.

There is one further activity in all areas, but especially historic ones, that planners can become involved in, which is "enhancement" – making a positive improvement to a locality. This does not, unfortunately, happen as often as it should but, nevertheless, can be very important when it does. Clearly, protection of existing buildings, and achieving high quality of design for new ones, are central to this, but they are not always sufficient to bring about an overall improvement in the appearance of an area. Painting existing woodwork in appropriate colours, adding trees and flowers together with sympathetically designed street furniture, can make a huge difference to the appearance of all localities, especially historic ones. This is achieved through positive negotiation rather than negative controls. Local businesses can have an important role to play here, in providing both money and political support, as they can benefit commercially from increased trade from more visitors and so reap the full benefit of an area's heritage potential.

Figure 7.7: Relating design to context. The building on the left is a large 19th century detached house, whereas the one on the right is a contemporary building forming part of a school. Note that it does not have an institutional appearance, as might have been expected, but has been designed to reflect its residential surroundings in Surbiton, SW London. (Tony Hall)

DECIDING SMALL MATTERS

How then can all these local decisions be made and on what basis? Frequent mention has been made above of the reactions of local people. These reactions will influence local political decisions both for deciding general policies and applications for planning permission. The planning process will, indeed, require local people to be asked for their views. However, it is important to understand that views of local people are not necessarily the same as "planning reasons" in a legal sense. The scope of planning argument is constrained by planning law, government policy and local policies.

Decisions affecting public areas should be guided by public policies within which these changes can be judged. These can be developed using the principles set out in Chapter 6, "The Medium Stuff", in particular "urban design". They should include not only the practical functions of the spaces but also pursuit of an attractive, if not beautiful, appearance and the retention of artefacts of long-term cultural value. What really helps, though, is having clear and strong political context and support.

When the issues are just between neighbours, and where there is no guidance from overall planning policy for the locality, it can be quite another matter. Neighbours as individuals may hold strong feelings. Skills in negotiation and arbitration may be required for planning officers. Sometimes there are general planning principles that have evolved as precedents that can be used. Each generation of planning practitioners passes on assumptions and guidance to the next. An example in the British context is the avoidance of over-looking of a neighbour's activities from next door's windows. One can find planners applying it even when there is no explicit policy about it in a plan. (With this particular example, as with other as-pects of neighbour relations, its importance can vary between differ-ent cultures and will not be the same in all countries.)

All the examples considered above are fairly small scale — houses, small shops. If we move on to larger buildings and their extensions, infill and change of use "all of the above" issues still apply only more so. It is not so much that additional factors come into play, or though that can be the case depending on circumstances, but that all the issues have a heightened importance when they apply on a much larger scale.

THE IMPORTANCE OF THE "SMALL STUFF"

To summarise, the argument for the role of planning in small-scale matters is the cumulative and knock-on effects of repeated deci-sions and the creation of precedents. The removal of an individual tree may not be seen as a big deal, but if this is repeated within an important setting, all this contribution to the overall setting may be lost. One, or even several, new houses may not make a signif-icant addition to traffic on a road but, if there was restricted road junction a short distance away, then there may be a local problem.

If the addition of a number of houses is repeated over a wide area over time, then a change in traffic levels can be expected. All these changes affect people's everyday lives. Decisions, therefore, about relatively small matters may need guiding by local, or even general, policies. What all the examples considered show is that, even if there is, regrettably, little progress in getting results with the "big stuff", there is still a great deal of work for the planning profession to do, and, by getting on with it, it can make a significant improvement to people's surroundings.

8

POLICIES AND DECISIONS – HOW A PLANNING SYSTEM WORKS

We have talked about why we need to have a planning system, and the issues that need to be decided when using it, but how are these matters to be managed in practice? How do you go about it? We said at the beginning that this book is not about current law and procedures (because they can vary a lot over time) but, nevertheless, there has to be a definite legal and administrative structure governing how decisions are made in planning. Even when methods of planning decision-making vary between different countries, and they can do significantly, there are, nevertheless, certain common characteristics.

An individual or organisation needs to apply for permission to carry out development. The decision made on whether to permit it has to be judged against public policy, usually in the form of a development plan. Such a plan may take a variety of forms within any given country, and there can be significant differences between the practices in different countries. The underlying implication is, though, the existence of a legal structure to regulate the whole system.

An important point needs to be made here. It is very easy for the public, and also some practitioners, to begin to see "the system" as what "planning" is or, at the very least, to feel planning should keep to its minimum legal requirements. This can be a sad and unfortunate outcome. Any proper planning process requires much discussion and negotiation. It is rarely just a mechanical matter of checking a proposal against regulations or a map. Planning as it ought to be is far more than what happens after an application for permission to develop has been made. Discussion and negotiation, both public and private, can take place between interested parties long before this stage and, in ideal circumstances, the legally required process should come towards the later, rather than the earlier, stages. Furthermore, it should be clear from the arguments at the beginning of this book that planning originally arose as a value-laden reaction to issues of public concern. The legal structure arose in response to this. This legal structure was, and is, a means to an end, not an end in itself.

There have to be "plans" and "policies" in order to guide decisions on specific proposals for development. "Plans" here refers to development plans which apply to particular areas of land, usually towns and cities, and set out where future development will be allowed, and not allowed, and often its type and quantity. Usually, they include maps but may also have policies setting out intention without specific locations saying what you must do if certain circumstances apply – a more "what if" or "criteria-based" approach. In some localities, these may be set out as "codes" – what to do in a long list of circumstances – forming either part of the development plan or a separate document. There can also be plans for very small areas, usually called "briefs", "frameworks" or "master plans", setting out in more detail the planning authority's requirements for sites where development is expected in the short term. Some may not be plans as commonly understood because they do not refer to particular areas of land but apply throughout a planning authority's jurisdiction. They may consist of general statements of intention, for example, those on local economic matters or design guides referring to the detailed treatment of buildings and their layout.

It should be clear from the whole tone of this book that planning is very political. Also, it is very public, unlike say medicine or social work, or even policing, where, although the professional activities are publicly and politically regulated, there are issues of client confidentiality. For planning, approval of plans and policies, and often of proposals for development, has to be given in public or, at least, made available for public scrutiny.

This brings us to the levels of government: central, local, regional and neighbourhoods. In some countries, planning powers exist only at one level of government, but in Britain, there are powers at a number of levels, all of which may have their own policies. Policy statements and decisions may be issued by the central government, taking precedence over local government policies, although most of the planning work is actually undertaken by local councils. In certain circumstances, design guides and briefs may be produced by village and neighbourhood organisations, although they do not possess normal planning powers, and then adopted by local councils.

THE BASIS FOR DECISIONS

When agreeing a local plan or policy, or deciding upon whether a particular proposal for development should be allowed, there is usually a set list of matters that have to be considered. Although details may vary from time to time, there is always a basic structure to such lists.

- Firstly, is it legal? Usually, this should be fairly straightforward matter.
- Secondly, is it in line with government policy? This may not be so straightforward, given the complexity of government statements and documents, but is very important.
- Thirdly, is it in line with the planning authority's existing development plans and other policy statements? For a large and complex proposal, this may not be as easy as it may first appear.

When deciding to approve a specific proposal, there can be significant differences between countries in the degree to which plans and policies are strictly binding on the planning authority or whether some leeway is allowed. In many countries, there is little, or no, discretion – it is clear whether or not, and if so, how, you are allowed to develop in a particular place, with no argument. On the other hand, in some other countries, especially Britain, there is a lot of room for debate about the merits of a proposal and the degree to which it may, or may not, be in line with planning policies. This is often referred to as a "discretionary" system.

CONSULTATION AND PARTICIPATION – BRINGING IN OTHERS

The decision-making process normally includes periods of "consultation", "participation" and "working together". Although these terms are sometimes used interchangeably, they are, in practice, quite different activities. Consultation can be achieved by the minimal activity of sending details to the consultee and then waiting for them to send back a response. Participation implies inviting another person or organisation to play a positive role in developing the policy and/ or making the decision. Working together is the most desirable and the most difficult to achieve in practice. It implies that the people and organisations involved will set up permanent, or semi-permanent, arrangements, in advance, for personnel to cooperate in preparing policies and making decisions on a regular basis. They do it because they see it as desirable as a result of the superior outcomes it produces. Indeed, quite a task.

In British practice, an application for planning permission should be followed by consultations with other departments of the local council, with a range of outside interest groups and individuals and with the public at large. If development is proposed for a particular site, it is possible to itemise all the stakeholders, users, neighbours, government bodies and so on, that have an interest in the proposal. This will reveal how much support this proposal has amongst these interest groups and the public which will be important knowledge for the local politicians. However, strictly speaking, conducting something like an opinion poll is not the purpose of the exercise. It is done to gain knowledge for two things:

- how individuals and groups might be personally affected in ways that may not have been foreseen and
- positive suggestions that may not have previously come to light.

Although such consultations are not meant to be a referendum on support for a proposal, it may sometimes seem like it. Local protest groups may find that they cannot prevail against decisions that will be taken on the "planning merits" of the development, albeit that these merits are defined by local and central government policy, which themselves are political decisions. Out of this may come a view on whether the proposal is "acceptable" and to what degree.

WORKING WITH OTHER PROFESSIONS AND ORGANISATIONS

Because planning covers such a wide range of built structures and human activities, it is inevitable that consultation and participation will involve a variety, and sometimes a significant number, of professions and organisations. Most planning decisions are made by local councils and worked on by officers within a planning department or equivalent, whatever name it may be called by. There will be many other parts of the council's operation outside of its planning department that need to be consulted and ideally worked with in partnership. The professions impinging on planning listed above will normally have their own departments and so, to start with, there has to be interdepartmental working within the local authority. For example, many decisions will involve roads and highway engineers. Some will involve parks and other open space, some social housing provision and so on. All of these may also touch on legal issues.

Indeed, one particular problem that affects planning more than many other activities is the close, and sometime ill-defined, boundary between planning as a profession and that of other professions. We are talking here not just about the closely related professions of architecture, landscape architecture, civil engineering, building and surveying but also the other professional areas of housing management, environmental health and the police. To take just one example, when dealing with proposals for a new restaurant or bar, with regard to possible noise from patrons and odours from cooking, there is an interface here with the environmental health profession. There is also the role of the legal profession, which underpins all planning activities. The line at which "planning" stops and other professions take over can be a very fuzzy one. It can sometimes be difficult to separate these professional boundaries and, indeed, there will be a need for co-operation. Consultations are always necessary, but the best solution may often be joint working between professionals, not just consultations between them.

Consultations and joint working with the local council are just the beginning of the planning officer's tasks. As already mentioned, there will often be significant organisations outside of the council to deal with. An applicant for planning permission may not just be an individual but a large firm, such as a property developer or retailer. There will also be public sector applicants such as hospitals, colleges and universities. In addition to the applicants themselves, there may be similar public and private sector organisations that may be affected by the proposal. There will also be community groups and departments of central government that may have a direct interest. At a minimum, for a large and complex application for planning permission there will be a long list of consultees. In the ideal situation, a planning authority would be positive and pro-active, working with outside organisations some time in advance, before an application is made.

POSITIVE POLICY

Most planning decision-making proceeds in the manner set out above. However, ideally this should not be all that happens. By itself, this is a passive, even negative, process. It can result in the "least bad" alternative being adopted rather the "most desirable". This not what professional planning need be about, or should be about, in all cases. There is scope for leadership and for the encouragement of development that can positively enhance a locality. Nearly all planning systems provide for development plans and other policy documents that can be used in a pro-active way. That this may not happen is no reason why it should not be made to happen. Potential issues between stakeholders can be worked out in advance. Physical and practical solutions to known problems, such as traffic conflicts, can be worked out. There is scope for vision about the scope for potential enhancement, such as the promotion of quality architecture and the restoration and re-use of historic buildings. Planning is at its best when it is positive and pro-active, taking a lead to make people's lives better.

APPEALING AGAINST DECISIONS

Because, in nearly all countries, planning is set up as part of a legal system, there is always provision for appeal to a court of law on the legality of a planning decision or planning document, usually in terms of whether the correct procedures were followed. Appeals on the content of a planning decision are another matter entirely, and there can be wide variation between different countries in what is allowed. In Britain, appeals are determined by the central government with the aid of a professional inspectorate. Appeals can be made only against failure to grant planning permission, and there is no provision for appeals by third parties against the grant of permission. The appeal is determined not just in terms of "good planning", or conformity with local planning policies, but conformity with the central government's current views on planning, thus providing the government with a way of enforcing its polices. It may surprise many British readers to discover that, in many countries, planning appeal to a higher level of government does not exist because it would be unconstitutional. In countries such as Germany and the USA, the constitution allocates separate powers and responsibilities to the different levels of government and a higher level cannot overrule a lower one on matters of planning. Many countries have procedures that lie between these extremes. For example, in Australia, appeals against local government planning decision are heard by special courts at state level, and third-party appeals are allowed. However, the Federal Government does not get involved.

THE BRITISH EXPERIENCE – A HISTORIC OVERVIEW

Planning systems are not fixed creations but evolve over time. There can be a continuous tension between what professionals may see as "good planning" and the social and political forces at work within society that impact upon it. This can, and has, result in progress in the long term, but it can also produce a circular process where debates and decisions repeat over time because of a failure to resolve the underlying issues. This can be illustrated by taking an overview of the British experience since the passing of the major planning legislation of the late 1940s.

The development plans required by the 1947 Town and Country Planning Act were called "maps" – County Maps and Town Maps – and there was meagre supporting text, particularly when compared to the content of later generations of plans. These maps showed the preferred land uses against which applications for planning permission were to be determined, which was in some detail for the Town Maps. This rather limited format should not be taken as necessarily representing planning thinking at the time – witness ideas behind the New Towns that were being designed at the same time. It was due more to the limitations of the legislators' approach. The moral here is that planning is much more than the system of laws and procedures used in any one time period. Development plans were to be drawn up by County Councils and had to be approved by the central government. They were then expected to be revised every five years. It soon became clear that this time scale was not going to be met. Plans took far longer to prepare than expected, and the government took even longer to approve them. It was the mid-to-late 1950s before most parts of the country were covered by a development plan. The best resourced and enthusiastic planning authorities had set to work on the first revision, but by the mid-1960s, only a limited number had the first revision of their plan fully approved.

It was clear that an improved development plan system was needed and there was debate about the form it should take. Positions in the argument started to emerge that continue to the present day. Politicians tend to blame the system for failure to deliver on housing numbers and other targets. Developers say that it is too complicated and that everything would go quicker if it were simplified, an idea also attractive to national politicians. On the other hand, local people (when are not themselves applicants for permission) want to see detailed supervision of development. Close control is popular at grass-root level. The overall problem in the 1960s was that then, as now, there was a lot of development taking place, particularly new houses, and there needed to be control over its location and design if was to be properly planned. Preparing and implementing such guidance required a complex system and lot of resources. A government report in 1965 advocated a two-tier approach, with an upper level of "county maps" and "urban structure maps" that would provide a broad framework of land uses (and thus hopefully quick to prepare) together with "action area" plans that would be very detailed but prepared only when and where development was imminent. In 1968 and 1971, the government introduced legislation requiring County

Councils to prepare "structure plans" with District Councils empowered to produce "local plans" as, and when, circumstances merited it. The structure plans that emerged were far more sophisticated than the previous "maps". They contained detailed written policies based largely on evidence. Although this mean that significant resources were required for their preparation, by the 1980s effective national coverage had been achieved, and these plans were being reviewed on a systematic basis.

The problem that persisted throughout the 1960s, 1970s and 1980s was how to have sufficient and effective plans, and other guidance, at a local level. Planning thinking, particularly in academic circles, during the 1960s and 1970s did not place much weight on the detailed planning and design of urban areas. The 1960s saw an emphasis on mathematical models for forecasting population, housing and traffic. The 1970s saw stress on the social and economic factors and the pursuit of social justice. Where great progress in planning practice made at this time was at the strategic level. The 1960s saw number of significant regional and sub-regional studies and the 1970s the emergence of a proper regional planning framework.

At the local level, although a number of planning authorities produced and adopted local plans, and went on to revise them and keep them up to date, such plans did not necessarily cover the whole of their areas and large parts of the country were completely without them. This created a rather peculiar situation when it came to deciding on planning permission. On what basis could the decisions be made in the absence of local policy? Moreover, there was a lot of building going on. In practice, the decision-making criteria came from the cumulative experience of the planning profession, within a strategic context set by central government policy, regional and structure plans. In much of the country, this lasted for 30 years. Although not a desirable situation, what it does show, amongst other things, is how planning as an activity is very much more than the system of plans and procedures applying at any given time.

In the early 1980s, the government tried to downplay the role of planning generally and control of design in particular. However, the planning profession still had to, and, by and large did, deal with pressing issues, particularly the increasing demand for more houses. In the late 1980s, there was a dramatic boom and bust in house prices and, for a range of pressing reasons, the government was forced into an about-turn on planning policy. It had to accept that there was a need for more dwellings and that a substantial proportion would be within urban areas and at higher densities. This would require fairly detailed guidance on the design and layout and full, national coverage by local plans. Following a new Act of Parliament in 1990, urban design found itself back at the centre of planning activity. A steady stream of national reports and guides began to be published, almost as though pent-up professional creativity had suddenly been released. At the local level, in addition to local plans, design guides and planning briefs for individual sites, which had always been possible, now become much more frequent. The new legislation not only introduced local plans that covered the whole of a planning authority's area but re-established the primacy of the plan in deciding applications for planning permission. However, the time and resources necessary to produce the plans meant, that it was going to be many years before anything approaching national coverage was to be achieved.

The first decades of the 21st century saw the government dismantle the provisions for strategic planning at the regional and sub-regional scale. First, structure plans were abolished and then regional planning. This left local plans as the principal vehicle for planning policy within the constraints of the policy statements issued by the central government. The debates and political pressures on the development plan framework that had been at work ever since the 1960s now focused upon them. In pursuit of a "simpler" (and, so it was hoped, quicker) planning system, changes by the central government to the local planning framework became more frequent. The distinction between "structure" and "action area" was now applied within a local plan framework. As in the previous decades, although a rational principle, this idea came up against the fact that in many parts of the country "action" was needed nearly everywhere and all the time. This required detailed local guidance and, with the frequent changes, the local development planning system became, in reality, more, not less, complex.

One new and very interesting innovation that took place in roughly the same period was the provision for development plans for very small areas, produced with a high degree of local participation.

Towards the end of the 1990s, "village design statements" started to appear promoted by local councils and then village plans instigated and produced by groups of local people. To have any force, they had to be adopted by the local council as supplementary planning guidance. In the early 21st century, the government actively encouraged production of "neighbourhood plans" by local groups. The idea was that these would not be local council initiatives but would arise from the commitment of local interests and individuals expressing the desires of a local "community". They would, however, have to go through a set approval procedure and be in general conformity with the local planning authority's development plan. Their production did, in practice, require a lot of time and other resources, and this tended to limit the number ultimately adopted. Once adopted, local people could be disappointed to discover that a neighbourhood plan did not mean local decision-making, much less a local inspectorate. In the British discretionary system, other factors could override the content of the plan when it came to particular, and perhaps controversial, decisions. Again, the moral of the story is that plans are not the whole planning system and this system is not, in itself, the whole of planning.

CONCLUSION

Planning can be a very difficult subject to get one's head around, much less to define it. It covers a very wide range of subject matter and seeks contributions from an equivalent range of other professions, such as law, architecture, surveying, civil engineering, economics, sociology – the list can go on and on. It also operates at a wide range of spatial scales, all the way from economic regions down to an individual tree. Moreover, as we have seen, all these topics and scales interact with one another. For convenience, we have tried to separate them out in the preceding chapters, but there are no really clear-cut divisions in practice. Most practitioners would maintain, and hopefully believe, that the whole is more than the sum of its parts and that planning is a distinctive profession in its own right. It gains its coherence and purpose from being problem focussed. It is there to address people's needs. To do this, it has to possess its own values. It is not or, rather, should not be, a dry mechanical operation. This means that it must, of necessity, interact with politics and government, again at a range of scales from parish and neighbourhood to central government. This perspective may seem over grand, but it arises from the problem-centred nature of planning, when this is properly addressed.

We have seen how contemporary planning had its origins in the problems of the 19th century industrial city, and some of these basic contradictions are still with us today. People move to the city to work because that is where the jobs are. Unfortunately, as they are all doing the same thing, the price of the land they are seeking to live on rises and they can find it difficult to afford something adequate. The better-off can afford to travel some way to work, and can therefore find land that is cheaper, but those that cannot do this are faced with difficulty in affording somewhere decent to live. There is a need to provide both sufficient and affordable houses in the right places and jobs in the right places. These need to be linked together with proper transport, water supply and sewers and to have sufficient schools and recreational facilities. Planning has offered solutions over the past 100 years, notably garden cities and new towns, where land is acquired at, or near to, existing use value and towns are built with all necessary facilities and infrastructure. Unfortunately, governments have not always been happy with the ideas underlying this and, as a result, proper solutions have not been implemented and matters of, say, sufficient housing have not always been properly solved.

Planning is also concerned with environmental issues. There are direct issues for urban areas of providing clean air, pure water, sewage and refuse disposal that go back to the origins of planning. These can now be combined with the benefits of walking and cycling for personal health to contribute to the idea of the "healthy city". They also have an impact on the countryside surrounding towns and cities – where is the water to come from and where is the waste to be disposed of? However, the issues in rural areas go way beyond the impact of adjacent urban areas. They contain activities that, unfortunately, compete with each other and can also change markedly over time. Rural areas produce food through farming and minerals through quarrying. On the other hand, people want areas of countryside protected not just from urban expansion but also from mineral extraction because what they see as its charm and appearance. Some areas need to be protected for their scientific interest. People also want to use the countryside for recreation and tourism. The latter generates income for the local inhabitants but conflicts with agricultural, scientific and all the other uses. As a result, rural planning requires complex and difficult decisions to be made, just as planning does in urban areas.

All the activities planning deals with are linked together by transport facilities. They not only facilitate movement but affect the location of these same activities. The use of motor vehicles for the transport of both people and goods encourage more movement and for uses to be located farther apart. Urban areas can spread out at low density. Motor vehicles, especially the private car, are very popular with their users because of their convenience and the opportunities for travel that they open up. The trouble is that there is just not the space to fit them all in if everybody used one. Although they are not going to be eliminated, limits on their use have to be planned-in and other ways of getting around, for example rail-based systems in urban areas, pursued. It has also been found that the pursuit of speed within urban areas is ultimately self-defeating, and environmental quality and the optimum layout of urban areas are best achieved through low-speed environments ensured by the appropriate design of streets.

Mention of physical design takes us on to another, and more successful, area of planning – placemaking, urban design and finding the best location of activities within urban areas. Although, for political reasons, complete solutions have rarely been achieved for the big issues, at what might be seen as the "medium level", there has been much more success. Planners have to consider at a local level the best location not just for homes and jobs but for schools, shops, community and recreational facilities and so on. The buildings that contain them also define urban spaces that people use – streets, parks and the like – and planning practice now contains much knowledge and expertise about how to do this successfully. It is not just a matter of appearances (although this is very important) but about personal safety and sociability. Placemaking is important for the conservation of the historic environment for the protection of heritage for benefit of future generations. This can also be significant for the local economy, particularly tourism, by encouraging visitors to spend their money in the locality. Promotion of tourist potential is just one element within a range of activities at this scale that can aid the local economy and regenerate areas that have fallen into economic decline.

Much of the actual work within a planning office, including that of local planning consultants, is often at a smaller scale still. The change of use of individual buildings, the construction of new ones in spaces within existing urban areas or by the replacement of existing ones, all has to be decided upon. More frequent still are what are called "householder" matters – extensions to houses, garages and so on. There is also the approval of alterations to historic buildings. There is also the protection of trees. Although minor in scale, all these small items contribute overall to the maintenance of the quality of the local environment. They are not only important for daily lives of individuals but, in aggregate, for the implementation of wider planning policy.

A planning system – legislation, provision for plans policies the granting or refusal of permission to develop – is a necessary requirement wherever in the world planning is practised. However, it is not the whole picture. It does not, in itself, define the content of planning. Development plans, and other policy documents, while essential in themselves, are, also, not the whole process. Decision-making relating to development requires not just consultation between the decision-makers, other agencies and the public at large but should, ideally, incorporate genuine participation and working together. Although a legal skeleton is essential, planning is a purposeful activity which should be defined by its values and its ability to put them into practice.

INDEX

Note: *Italic* page numbers refer to figures.

Lightning Source UK Ltd.
Milton Keynes UK
UKHW020727181222
414076UK00028B/471